Managing the Euro Crisis

The financial crisis posed new challenges for the administrations of Eurozone countries, including: How to respect EU obligations when the economy is under stress? How to improve the overall implementation of EU policies and domestic reforms? How to negotiate effectively with the Troika and then quickly and efficiently fulfil the requirements of the Memoranda of Understanding?

This volume offers the first analysis of EU coordination by national executives in the light of the legal and political consequences of the crisis, using case studies of five severely affected Member States: Cyprus, Greece, Ireland, Italy, and Portugal. It examines from an interdisciplinary perspective how they have adapted their coordination systems since the outbreak of the crisis, shedding light on the adjustments undertaken by domestic administrations.

The comparison reveals that in this process Prime Ministers and Ministers of Finance were empowered in a common shift towards the centralization of EU coordination.

Sabrina Ragone is an associate professor of comparative law at the University of Bologna. Previously, she was a senior research fellow at the Max Planck Institute for Comparative Public Law and International Law in Heidelberg and at the Center for Political and Constitutional Studies in Madrid. She has held positions as a researcher, lecturer and visiting professor in several academic institutions in France, Germany, Italy and Spain, as well as in Latin America and the United States. Her scholarship focuses on legal comparison intersecting constitutional law and the distribution of powers within domestic institutions.

Routledge Research in EU Law

Available titles in this series include:

Global Data Protection in the Field of Law Enforcement
An EU Perspective
Cristina Blasi Casagran

The Judge and the Proportionate Use of Discretion
A Comparative Administrative Law Study
Sofia Ranchordás and Boudewijn de Waard

The Greening of European Business under EU Law
Taking Article 11 TFEU Seriously
Beate Sjåfjell and Anja Wiesbrock

The Habitats Directive in its EU Environmental Context
European Nature's Best Hope?
Charles-Hubert Born, An Cliquet, Hendrik Schoukens, Delphine Misonne, and Geert Van Hoorick

Towards a System of European Criminal Justice
The Problem of Admissibility of Evidence
Andrea Ryan

The Legal Order of the European Union
The Institutional Role of the European Court of Justice
Timothy Moorhead

https://www.routledge.com/Routledge-Research-in-EU-Law/book-series/ROUTEULAW

Managing the Euro Crisis

National EU Policy Coordination in the Debtor Countries

Edited by Sabrina Ragone

Routledge
Taylor & Francis Group
LONDON AND NEW YORK

First published 2018 by Routledge

2 Park Square, Milton Park, Abingdon, Oxfordshire OX14 4RN
52 Vanderbilt Avenue, New York, NY 10017

Routledge is an imprint of the Taylor & Francis Group, an informa business

First issued in paperback 2019

British Library Cataloguing in Publication Data
A catalogue record for this book is available from the British Library

Library of Congress Cataloging in Publication Data
A catalog record for this book has been requested

ISBN: 978-1-138-12379-3 (hbk)
ISBN: 978-0-367-87551-1 (pbk)

Typeset in Galliard
by Keystroke, Neville Lodge, Tettenhall, Wolverhampton

Managing the Euro Crisis

National EU Policy Coordination in the Debtor Countries

Edited by Sabrina Ragone

Routledge
Taylor & Francis Group
LONDON AND NEW YORK

First published 2018 by Routledge

2 Park Square, Milton Park, Abingdon, Oxfordshire OX14 4RN
52 Vanderbilt Avenue, New York, NY 10017

Routledge is an imprint of the Taylor & Francis Group, an informa business

First issued in paperback 2019

British Library Cataloguing in Publication Data
A catalogue record for this book is available from the British Library

Library of Congress Cataloging in Publication Data
A catalog record for this book has been requested

ISBN: 978-1-138-12379-3 (hbk)
ISBN: 978-0-367-87551-1 (pbk)

Typeset in Galliard
by Keystroke, Neville Lodge, Tettenhall, Wolverhampton

Contents

List of illustrations

Figures

Tables

Notes on contributors

Brigid Laffan is Director and Professor at the Robert Schuman Centre for Advanced Studies, European University Institute (EUI), Florence.

José Magone is Professor of Regional and Global Governance at the Berlin School of Economics and Law.

Adonis Pegasiou is an Adjunct Lecturer of Political Science at the University of Cyprus.

Sabrina Ragone is Associate Professor of Comparative Law at the University of Bologna.

Calliope Spanou is Professor of Administrative Science and Public Administration at the National and Kapodistrian University of Athens.

1 Introduction

Sabrina Ragone

1 The topic

The topic of this volume is the national EU policy coordination in the countries most severely affected by the Eurozone financial and debt crisis. This is a highly salient political and legal issue with important policy implications that has not yet been addressed in the scholarship.

In general terms, the research on the topic of how Member States manage their EU policy process at home and how they organize their negotiations in Brussels deserves to be updated – not only because national governments have historically been central actors in the process of integration but also because of its contemporary relevance. The deepening of integration in the last decade – through the Lisbon Treaty – and the enlargement – moving from 15 to 28 members within a few years – require fresh attention to the relationship between the EU and its Member States. National Parliaments as well as Regions and national Courts are increasingly participating in this relationship, although the national executives remain the fundamental axes.

The domestic coordination of European policies is one of the paramount angles from which scholars can analyse both the influences of Member States on EU law-making processes and the Europeanization of national administrations. The national coordination system consists of different mechanisms aiming at integrating the activities of ministries (and, depending on the case, also domestic Parliaments and/or Regions) and solving potential conflicts. Those mechanisms come into play in two distinct moments of the EU decision-making process: in the bottom-up or ascending phase, when every government formulates the position it will hold, defend, and negotiate within the European institutions and in the top-down or descending phase, when national authorities transpose and implement directives and other decisions adopted at the European level. The instruments of coordination are of a legal and administrative nature, but also include practices; therefore, they can be better examined using an interdisciplinary approach that crosses legal and political studies.

This volume aims to combine the attention given to the topic of national EU policy coordination systems with another unquestionably relevant object of study: the impact of the current crisis in the most stressed countries of the Eurozone.

Several years of crisis have brought about important legal and political changes in a group of Member States that, although diverging in many aspects, share a similar economic and political weakening within the EU – a matter of fact that is captured in the controversial labels of 'debtor' or even 'peripheral' countries vis-à-vis 'creditor' and supposedly 'central' states. From this perspective, the selected case studies include Cyprus, Greece, Ireland, Italy, and Portugal.

The list includes both countries that have signed Memoranda of Understanding (MoUs) with the so-called 'Troika' (International Monetary Fund – IMF, European Central Bank – ECB, and European Commission) to deal with the implementation of the bail-out and one country that has not. This was a key variable in the research project. Having signed a MoU had, in principle, a paramount impact on the domestic coordination.

A brief description of the context will aid our understanding of why these countries were selected. While Greece formally requested and received the first rescue package in spring 2010, the rating agencies were downgrading other countries' credit ratings (a phenomenon that would repeat itself over the course of several months), generating panic in the financial markets. Meanwhile, the Irish crisis originated from the decision of the Irish Government to guarantee the liabilities of the country's main banks; a few months after Greece, Ireland also requested assistance from the EU and the IMF. In 2011, it was Portugal's turn to receive, through the European Financial Stability Mechanism (EFSM) and the European Financial Stability Facility (EFSF), a rescue package financed by the IMF and the EU.

In November 2012, Cyprus also sought recourse to the EU and IMF to sanitize its banking system and its deteriorating public finances. Despite gradual downgrades in the credit rating and increases in bond interest rates, Italy was not subject to a rescue package. Nevertheless, over the past few years Italian governments have been inclined and/or somehow forced to adopt austerity measures and structural reforms in order to overcome the crisis.

The described situation, therefore, features an element of absolute novelty: the domestic coordination of European policies must be modified in order to adapt to the interaction with the Troika during the implementation of MoU-prescribed measures that are conditional to the rescue packages. In cases in which there was no bail-out (like Italy), the need to implement radical adjustments and austerity measures also affected the national system of EU policy-making.

2 An innovative approach

The existing literature on these two issues (the national coordination of EU policies and the financial crisis) lets us maximize the theoretical robustness of this volume. Nevertheless, the two research lines have not intersected so far.

The scholarship on EU coordination mainly dates back to the 1990s, when several works on Europeanization and the relation between the Member States and the EU were published. The main reference for the topic of EU policy coordination was authored by Kassim, Peters and Wright in 2000, who analysed nine cases.

The recent works on the same issue only address a few countries and adopt a very specific point of view. For instance, Jordan and Schout 2006 studied Germany, the Netherlands, and the UK with reference to environmental policies; and S. Baroncelli 2008 studied Spain, Germany, Austria, and Italy with a focus on the rule-making process in general. Also, the special issue edited by Kassim and Le Galès in 2010 was based on different policies, as was Bulmer and Lequesne 2005. There are now more studies on the new Eastern and central European Member States, such as Dimitrova and Toshkov 2007 or Gärtner, Hörner and Obholzer 2011.

In this respect, a couple of years ago, Kassim underlined the relevance of the Eastern European group of Member States as a case study (Kassim 2015). It is true that the new Member States have recently represented an interesting example of imitation of models and adaptation of the administrations existing before the accession to the EU. However, no comprehensive analysis has been devoted so far to the 'debtor countries' as a group, which is characterized by common problems and thus is potentially subject both to adaptation and imitation of foreign models.

As was mentioned, the volume aims to link the matter of EU coordination by domestic executives to the consequences of the financial crisis in order to explore whether and how the negative economic situation and its legal assessment have provoked changes in the coordination mechanisms. The connection between national EU policy-making and the crisis has not been covered by the literature so far. Of course, a great deal has been published on the Eurozone crisis, mostly in journal articles, but current studies on the effects of the crisis have not focused on this specific aspect.

Some features indirectly connected to the topic have been addressed, such as the constitutional effects of the crisis at the European and national level (see, for example, Tuori and Tuori 2013, or the special issue of the *European*

Law Journal, n. 2, 2014). At the same time, the decision-making process adopted inside the EU has been critically analysed (see de Witte, Heritier, and Trechsel 2013), as well as the role of the ECB. At the national level, particular attention has been devoted to the constitutional amendments and legal reforms (see Contiades 2013) that are somehow related to the crisis.

Combining the two perspectives, this volume settles on original criteria, both in the selection of the case studies and in the choice of the perspective on the financial crisis, since internal side-effects have been studied in different directions. The coordination mechanisms put in place due to the bail-out packages of the Troika is also a topic with which the academic literature has barely dealt.

3 Methodological framework

The approach of the volume combines legal and political issues and is both empirical and theoretical. The chapters assess whether the Eurozone crisis was a critical juncture that transformed the national EU policy coordination system in each case study, and, if this was the case, what kind of changes took place (Capoccia and Kelemen 2007).

The perspective is comparative as well. Since the case studies present different systems of coordination that evolved over time in each State respectively, the volume takes into consideration two dimensions of comparison: the synchronic (between Member States during the crisis) and the diachronic (evolution of the EU coordination systems over time within each State).

To do so, each chapter puts forward a reconstruction of the legal (law in the books) and the political (law in action) framework in each country in order to determine what changes have taken place since the outbreak of the crisis and whether there has been a diffusion of certain models and an emergence of common patterns.

Of course, this central question is connected to many other analytical subquestions: Have new structures of coordination been created? Did certain central actors in the core executive (Prime Ministers, Ministers of Finance, Ministers of Foreign Affairs) gain or lose importance due to the crisis? What role did Parliaments play? Have the Member States' negotiation approaches in Brussels changed and become more or less selective? Are there differences between countries that received rescue packages and those that did not? Are there common tendencies? Which other domestic factors (linked to the political and administrative systems) can explain similarities and divergences?

All these questions have a remarkable theoretical relevance. The volume uses concepts and hypotheses derived from constitutional and administrative scholarship as well as new institutionalism, including both its different general variants (historical, rational choice, sociological) and its specific applications to the EU (particularly, Europeanization and EU governance approaches). For example, the research assesses whether the national coordination processes have become more centralized or, on the contrary, are still decentralized because traditional sectoral policy networks have been able to resist centralization.

In addition to this, the study considers to what extent the structural reforms introduced were intended by the national core executives or rather imposed from outside without the relevant domestic complicity. The question of whether 'debtor' Member States changed the focus of their national EU policy-making systems to prioritize effective 'downloading' over 'uploading' ambitions will be addressed as well.

4 The case studies – a brief introduction to the chapters

Each chapter first provides insights into the domestic coordination of EU policy since the Member State's accession and its incremental adaptation over the years to developments at the European level. It then highlights how the political and administrative systems reacted and adapted as the country was subject to MoU conditionality and/or under pressure due to its financial situation.

The first case study is Greece (Chapter 2). Calliope Spanou demonstrates how the domestic political-administrative system reacted to the new conditions during the crisis. Greece and its international creditors (the 'Troika'; later the 'Quartet') adopted three MoUs under the Economic Adjustment Programme (EAP). This determined a new policy environment, shaped by the so-called loan conditionality. The MoUs required the implementation of numerous reform measures for the continuation of financial assistance.

Many of the reforms were connected to the implementation of certain EU directives. Therefore, the embedding of EU policies within the requirements of the MoU provided the link between MoU implementation and national EU coordination. To face the MoU-imposed challenges, the system progressively adjusted, through gradual and informal means, within the limits and potentials of its capacities and institutional legacies.

Albeit no major institutional reform in terms of specialized EU coordination structures emerged, the urgency of fulfilling MoU requirements and their emphasis on economic and fiscal adjustments had a significant impact on the domestic political-administrative system – principally the *de facto* rise of the Ministry of Finance (MF) as the lead ministry. MoU 'prior actions' led to a new selective prioritization of EU policies, mainly in the form of economic and fiscal directives, and, thereby, to a shift of the centre of gravity from the Ministry of Foreign Affairs (MFA) towards the MF.

Furthermore, the critical difference between the usual EU procedures and the MoU-implementation scheme was that the latter was constrained by the expectation of immediate, predefined results, whereas the former always offers opportunity to debate and influence the outcome. This divergence in procedures explains the gradual development of the MoU's own monitoring and coordination mechanisms, which brought new actors to Greece.

Spanou clarifies how the fulfilment of the MoUs required new overarching coordination capacity that the MF with its resources was equipped to provide. Thus, the instrument of conditionality triggered the development of a new MF-led centralized, positive, and selective domestic coordination system of EU policies. Essentially, the policy environment caused the rise of three actors: the Minister of Finance, the SOE President (the SOE is the Council for Economic Advice attached to the MF), and the PM.

The MoU predefined tools for recovery brought to the fore the MF's new preeminent role that strengthened its status vis-à-vis other ministries, effectively sidelining other domestic institutions and actors (the MFA, sectoral ministries, but also Parliament). In effect, the larger the volume of Eurozone requirements, the lower the involvement of other ministries, particularly the MFA. Further-more, the MoU prioritized certain EU policies over others, which effectively sidelined some EU legislation. At times, relevant EU standards were neglected if in conflict with obligations stemming from the MoUs.

Brigid Laffan deals with the case of Ireland (Chapter 3), which became a programme country (Economic Adjustment Programme, EAP) and signed a MoU with its international creditors in November 2010. Contrary to Greece, the MoU in the Irish case was largely based on a domestically elaborated plan for economic recovery. The State successfully exited the bail-out programme in December 2013, not least due to the political-administrative system's adaptability, flexibility, and focus on core issues.

In Ireland, EU policy coordination follows a centralized scheme that is managed by the core executive. The author considers that it consists of the 'Holy Trinity' or hub of EU management (the MFA, the MF, and the Office of the PM), the inner core (ministries for whose work EU policies are central), and the outer circle of core-executive management (ministries that deal with EU business to lesser degrees.

Over the years, the ever-increasing task of managing EU business led to developments in the existing structures rather than to new institutions. The dominance of the executive in the management of EU business not only favoured centralized decision-making but also practically sidelined the role of Parliament. Following the critical juncture of the Nice Treaty referendum in 2001, the Government set out to remedy the limited role of Parliament in monitoring EU policy and developed a new system of enhanced parliamentary scrutiny.

When Ireland became a programme country, the Government's response was mainly directed towards repairing Ireland's international reputation and further strengthening the core executive by introducing institutional and personnel changes. Bringing in new staff was meant to ensure that highly competent personnel assumed the posts of senior civil servants.

Laffan emphasizes that an important institutional change was the division of the MF into a Ministry of Finance and a Ministry of Public Expenditure and Reform. Further, an Economic Management Council (EMC) emerged as the core strategist and coordinator to fulfil MoU requirements and move beyond the bail-out. In sum, the new Ministry of Public Expenditure and Reform, the Ministry of Finance, and the Office of the PM became the new 'Holy Trinity' in charge of managing the programme and engaging with the Troika and the EU through the EMC.

José Magone attends to the situation in Portugal (Chapter 4), where the political class regarded the bail-out conditions of the MoU as an interference with its socio-economic sovereignty; thus, it sought to implement the reforms and complete the programme successfully and quickly (2011–2014) in order to recover national sovereignty.

As the author explains, the financial crisis did not represent the first occasion on which the country had experienced economic problems. Nevertheless, the MFA-led system of EU policy coordination had remained simple and efficient. Being rather centralized and selective in terms of policy-making, the system used to focus on issues of national strategic importance, and Portugal has overall been an agenda-and-rule-taker.

The national liaison structure with the EU is part of the core executive and comprises several institutions that, over time, underwent some restructuring and renaming, and are located within the traditional MFA-led policy coordination system. Overall, the structures for coordinating EU policy remained quite stable despite governmental and economic instability. The crisis posed new challenges for the political-administrative system and led to slight deviations from the existing structures of EU policy coordination. As Magone clarifies, the innovative scheme of coordination took the form of a temporary taskforce. Most work related to the adjustment programme fell under the responsibility of the Office of the PM and the MF, who worked closely with this taskforce (the so-called ESAME).

Chapter 5 is devoted to the case of Cyprus. Adonis Pegasiou reconstructs why all attempts to create permanent EU coordination mechanisms have failed until now, however, the MoU to secure financial assistance from the Troika has successfully been implemented. The rigid institutional setting and interinstitutional rivalries are held responsible for the reliance on the creation of *ad hoc* mechanisms.

Pegasiou identifies different critical junctures at which a permanent EU Affairs coordination mechanism could have been set up. The first occurred with the EU accession negotiations that former President Vassiliou was appointed to lead in 1998. Then, an attempt by the President in 2006 to create an EU Office under his authority was overturned. A third juncture was in 2008, when elected President Christofias created a 'team', led by A. Moleskis, to prepare Cyprus for the Presidency of the Council. Again, the revival of negotiation about the country's division monopolized the Government's agenda and delayed the creation of a permanent coordination service. With the international financial crisis and social unrest, a political consensus was becoming impossible. In 2011, Moleskis was replaced by a non-political figure whose mandate was set to expire with the end of Cyprus's EU Presidency.

When the financial crisis hit, Cyprus had no established coordination mechanism to negotiate with the Troika, but an agreement was quickly found once the new President was elected in February 2013. A specialized coordination mechanism was set up to monitor the short-run implementation of the MoU under the supervision of the MF. The Government could implement the MoU measures thanks to the MF's effective mediating between Parliament and the Troika.

A recent attempt to establish an EU coordination permanent mechanism under the control of the MFA failed again due to several factors, among them the non-political appointment of the post, the reluctance to cooperate of other ministries, and the lack of personnel. Added to that, the Government seemed indifferent to its failure. Cyprus thus continues to rely on targeted arrangements with the Government's spokesman mediating between the involved ministries.

While all the countries mentioned above had to face bail-out packages, Italy represents a counter-part to these case studies. In Chapter 6, I investigate whether the evolution of domestic EU coordination mechanisms resulted from a critical juncture during the financial crisis or rather from domestic changes. Put in a diachronic perspective, the national system progressively deepened the core executive's role, especially the PM's, in the procedures, while also multiplying specialized actors and, more recently, enhancing the role of Parliament and Regions.

Contrary to previous scholarship, I identify three phases; the first centred around the national Government and, above all, the MFA; the second around the establishment of a Department for Coordination of Community Policies (now DEP) inside the Office of the PM; and the third around the reforms of 2005 and 2012, which introduced preparatory bodies and adapted the mechanisms to the Treaty of Lisbon.

Even with the creation of the DEP in 1987 as a main coordination instrument, the MFA kept an important role in the EU's Common Foreign and Security Policy as well as the institutional linkage with the Permanent Representation in Brussels. To a greater degree, the Ministry of Economy and Finance (MEF) has gained a leading role regarding the economic policies, and that was particularly clear during the crisis. This has not hindered progress towards concentration of the tasks into the hands of the PM.

The chapter on Italy critically reconstructs the functioning of the coordination bodies. The DEP coordinates all levels of EU decision-making and its actors and monitors the negotiations in collaboration with the MFA. An Interministerial EU Committee (CIAE) supervises the coordination of political and strategic priorities of the Italian positions as well as the fulfilment of EU obligations. Since 2014 the CIAE has met on a regular basis and can rely on the Technical Evaluation Committee (CTV) for the preparation of its meetings and coordination of the participating actors.

Participation of Parliament has increased, thanks to the legal reforms passed in 2005 and, more importantly, in 2012. Regions have also reinforced their position. They are now more active in the CIAE as well as in scrutinizing the executive powers and the EU to maintain the subsidiarity principle.

Overall, Italy adopted and maintained a comprehensive approach in its attempt to influence the outcome of EU decision-making; however, its decentralized vision may well have recently been reversed according to my reconstruction. Since 2014, the expansion of the PM's power, which has been supported but not triggered by the crisis, has shifted the balance towards centralization while keeping a quite stable position for the MFA and MEF and at the same time strengthening the CIAE's coordination mission.

5 Acknowledgements

While treading the path that led to this book, we relied on the collaboration of several institutions which believed in the project.

The first acknowledgement goes to the CEPC (Centro de Estudios Políticos y Constitucionales) in Madrid, one of Spain's leading research centres. Thanks to CEPC's funding and the support of the deputy director for research, Prof. Isabel Wences, I carried out a project between 2012 and 2015 that analysed the role of domestic executives in the coordination of Europeanized policies and the EU's institutional scene.

The second acknowledgement goes to the Real Instituto Elcano, also situated in Madrid, which during the same period launched a project on this issue; it focused on the Spanish position in the EU decision-making process and its ability to both influence Brussels and successfully implement EU directives. We refer back to the results of that project concerning the case of Spain; it would represent a complementary case study situated between the ones analysed in this book, since the Spanish State submitted to a partial bail-out.

Both institutions sponsored a workshop in June 2014 entitled 'How to Influence Brussels in Times of Crisis: A Comparative Analysis of EU Policy-making and Coordination by Peripheral Member States', in which many of the authors of this volume presented the initial results of their research concerning the effects of the crisis on national coordination mechanisms.

More recently, the project has been supported, thanks to the director, Prof. Armin von Bogdandy, by the Max Planck Institute for Comparative Public Law and International Law (MPIL), Heidelberg. It has been integrated into the research titled 'Structural Transformation of Public Law', which is funded by the *Deutsche Forschungsgemeinschaft* (Leibniz Project) and which I am currently coordinating.

Special thanks go to all public officers who took the time to answer questions and share their knowledge and experience to improve the research. Thanks to Theodor Shulman, Klara Hillmann, and Anne Blickhan for their invaluable collaboration during the drafting, correction, and finalizing of the texts. Finally, I express my infinite gratitude to my colleagues from the CEPC and the MPIL who helped me to sharpen the arguments and advance the research. All the mistakes remain mine and my fellow partners' in this academic enterprise.

Bibliography

Baroncelli S. (ed.) (2008), *Il ruolo del Governo nella formazione e applicazione del diritto dell'Unione europea. Le peculiarità di un sistema costituzionale multilivello*, Turin, Giappichelli.

Bulmer S. and Lequesne C. (2005), *The Member States of the European Union*, Oxford, Oxford University Press.

Capoccia G. and Kelemen R.D. (2007), 'The Study of Critical Junctures: Theory, Narrative, and Counterfactuals in Historical Institutionalism', 59 *World Politics* (3) (341–369).

Contiades X. (ed.) (2013), *Constitutions in the Global Financial Crisis. A Comparative Analysis*, Farnham, Ashgate.

De Witte B., Heritier A. and Trechsel A. (eds.) (2013), *The Euro Crisis and the State of European Democracy: Contributions from the 2012 EUDO Dissemination Conference*, Florence, European University Institute.

Dimitrova A. and Toshkov D. (2007), 'The Dynamics of Domestic Coordination of EU Policy in the New Member States: Impossible to Lock In?', 30 *West European Politics* (5) (961–986).

Gärtner L., Hörner J. and Obholzer L. (2011), 'Coordination of EU Policy: A Comparative Study of the Twelve "New" Member States', 7 *Journal of Contemporary European Research* (1) (77–100).

Jordan A. and Schout A. (2006), *The Coordination of the European Union. Exploring the Capacities of Networked Governance*, Oxford, Oxford University Press.

Kassim H. (2015) 'The National Coordination of EU Policy', in Magone J. (ed.), *Routledge Handbook of European Politics*, London, Routledge (686–707).

Kassim H. and Le Galès P. (2010), 'Governing the European Union. Policy Instruments in a Multi-Level Polity', 33 *West European Politics* (1) (1–21).

Kassim H., Peters B. G. and Wright V. (eds.) (2000), *The National Co-ordination of EU Policy. The Domestic Level*, Oxford, Oxford University Press.

Tuori K. and Tuori K. (2013), *The Eurozone Crisis, A Constitutional Analysis*, Cambridge, Cambridge University Press.

2 EU coordination in Greece

'Forced' Europeanization under the MoU?

Calliope Spanou

1 Introduction

The Greek sovereign debt crisis and the subsequent monitoring by the Troika of institutional lenders (International Monetary Fund [IMF], European Central Bank [ECB], and European Commission) have been game changers for the domestic political-administrative system. The Troika and the adoption of the first Memorandum of Understanding (MoU) in 2010 added an additional layer to the domestic system of policy-making. More importantly, they shaped a new policy environment: domestic political actors and governmental institutions found themselves embedded in a new set of opportunities and risks, not least because of the restrictions imposed on their day-to-day operational sovereignty.

The measures agreed upon with the Troika shaped reform priorities that focused on policy areas included in the MoU as loan conditionalities, so-called 'prior actions', which are subject to constant supervision. Contrary to Dimitrova and Toshkov (2007, 977), conditionality as a policy instrument does not operate merely as (sometimes beneficial) external pressure. It rather represents an attempt to penetrate the political-administrative system. Next to the 'administrative fusion' and soft techniques of Europeanization, this has been a lever to indirectly gain control over the domestic system.

Loan conditionalities included the implementation of selected EU policies. They eventually affected the domestic EU policy coordination system and its priorities. The main questions regarding any development in EU coordination are: Does the MoU constitute a critical juncture that triggers institutional reform? How did the MoU implementation interact with the EU policy coordination system and what are possible adjustments?

The chapter starts with a brief overview of the general features of the Greek coordination of EU policies before discussing the changes brought about by the crisis, the implementation of the MoU, and their impact on the coordination system itself.

2 Basic features of the EU policy coordination system

Greece is a parliamentary democracy where the position of the Prime Minister (*prothypourgós, πρωθυπουργός*, PM) is considered politically strong. The political-administrative system is, however, characterized by a low degree of integration and weak capacity of its politically dominated bureaucracy. Legalism and a strong tendency towards detailed rules contrast sharply with strong informal aspects of administrative operation and implementation gaps.

Decentralization, fragmentation, and a high degree of informality have been the longstanding features of the domestic coordination of EU policy. The regulation on information and coordination is minimal, in particular at the decision stage of the EU policy process. Informal arrangements compensate – to some extent – the deficient central coordination mechanisms. Rather than relying on solid institutionalized structures and processes, valuable human capital is used, with all the advantages and disadvantages this may bring in terms of stability and institutional memory (Spanou 2003).

Generally, the locus for horizontal policy coordination (Peters 1998, 28 ff.) within the core executive may be: a) the PM, since the political responsibility in parliamentary regimes lies with him/her; b) the cabinet and its committees, the institution aptly tasked with the management of crosscutting issues; and c) central public agencies, such as the Ministry of Foreign Affairs (MFA) or the Ministry of Economic Affairs (MEA) and/or the Ministry of Finance (MF).

2.1 Two lead ministries

From the beginning of Greece's EU membership (1981), domestic coordination of European policies was assigned to two lead ministries: the MFA and the MEA. This arrangement (law 1104/1980) survived until recently. It involved a network-type arrangement around these two lead ministries. In the case of the lead-agency strategy, agreements must be developed cooperatively (Peters 1998, 38) to avoid competition and centrifugal tendencies that undermine coordination. Both lead ministries lacked particular power over sectoral ministries and both faced similar resistance in this regard.

2.1.1 Outward representation: MFA-led

The MFA was entrusted with the 'outward representation' of the country in the European Communities (later EU) in cooperation with other ministries and agencies. The political leadership of the MFA often comprised an alternate or a junior Minister of European Affairs, and one of the three posts of Secretary General (SG) was dedicated to European Affairs. The scope of competence of the (politically appointed) SG of European Affairs varies depending on the division of labour with the alternate or junior Minister but also with the permanent SG of the MFA, who is a career diplomat.

The MFA prepares for the General Affairs Council and the European Council. Beyond the political aspects of EU membership, this Ministry has a mission of intersectoral coordination in the planning, implementation, and evaluation of the European policy, which is explicitly mentioned in its statute (law 3566/2007). At the administrative level, this role is ensured by the Directorate General (DG) of EU Affairs, headed by a diplomat. A special legal service under the direct authority of the Minister comprises a European Law Division responsible for monitoring legal transposition and transgressions of Community law (ENY in the Greek abbreviation). In principle, the MFA is the only transmission channel for national positions on sectoral issues to the Brussels-based Permanent Representation.

However, the coordinating role and ambition of the MFA is uneven with regard to different policy sectors. 'External relations' are certainly its privileged area of intervention (Ioakimidis 1993, 219) and highly political issues are generally better prepared and coordinated (Spanou 2001). As to the rest, its coordination ambitions tend to be rather modest and of a pragmatic nature: it ensures 'negative coordination' when it detects visible inconsistencies between sectoral positions in view of the Committee of Permanent Representatives (COREPER).

The technocratic and complex character, and the volume of many economic and sectoral issues, as well as the lack of corresponding expert resources limit the ambitions of the MFA. The most obvious examples are economic coordination and the 'singular' autonomy of the Ministry of National Economy (Ioakimidis 1993, 220) as well as Agriculture – an 'independent kingdom' in the words of a former SG. For instance, the MFA forwards positions (that were transferred from the MEA to the MFA) to the Permanent Representation without any comment – the MFA conducts its coordination role 'at a distance'.

Coordination consists in following the agenda of the Council and knowing the positions to be presented, without necessarily having followed their elaboration. Sectoral ministries are entitled to a wide discretion in shaping their positions but they also tend to develop their own links and direct communication channels with the Permanent Representation. This is 'tolerated' on the condition that it is carried out in cooperation with the MFA when preparing the agenda of the COREPER and transferring guidelines and instructions to the Permanent Representation's *ad hoc* meetings.

The Permanent Representation as an external service of the MFA corresponds primarily to the mission of 'outward representation'. It is headed by an ambassador (the Permanent Representative), whose career trajectory may not necessarily focus on EU issues. The staff for the most part comprises MFA diplomats and experts, but it also includes representatives of all other ministries (Spanou 2001; Passas and Petraki 2009), who have direct informal contacts with, and receive guidelines and instructions from, their corresponding ministries. Economic issues are gathered in the economic and financial policy unit of the Permanent Representation under the responsibility of the economic adviser, a high-ranking official, who symbolizes the extension of the lead ministry in economic coordination (*infra*).

Downstream formal communication transits through the Permanent Representation to the MFA and the relevant ministry, whereas for upstream formal communication, sectoral ministries inform the MFA and the Permanent Representation simultaneously. Both in case of interministerial conflicts and in case of major issues, the Permanent Representative alerts the MFA, which then intervenes in order to ensure *ad hoc* (negative) coordination. The MFA is therefore often involved at a later stage in the negotiation process, while its coordinating effort is confronted with the insufficient or late preparation of sectoral positions and (or because of) the lack of clear sectoral priorities (Spanou 2000 and 2001).

2.1.2 Economic coordination

After Greece's accession to the European Communities (ECs), the MEA[1] was entrusted with domestic economic coordination, i.e. the mission to plan and coordinate economic development in the framework of the ECs. Its competences extended to the Economic and Financial Affairs Council (ECOFIN) issues and the implementation of Community support frameworks. Most important was its Directorate of Relations with the ECs/EU, which was responsible for the preparation and representation of the country in the European Council of Ministers. Furthermore, an office of legal ECs/EU issues was entrusted with the monitoring and coordination of both the transposition and the implementation of European legislation, while the MEA had to countersign all transposition acts.

A Council of Economic Experts (SOE in the Greek abbreviation)[2] attached to the Ministry was set up in 1987 to assume an advisory role in economic policy, i.e. to issue recommendations for the formulation of economic policy and the promotion of the necessary structural reforms. The SOE's formal tasks, as specified in law 1682/1987, did not specifically refer to the EU; however, with the Europeanization of economic policy, the SOE undertook a major role in EU issues, a role that extended far beyond mere expert advice. Combining an institutionalized political character with expertise strengthened the economic expertise of the MEA.

The President of the SOE represents the Minister in the Economic Policy Committee, the Economic and Financial Committee, and the working groups of the Council of Ministers of the EU. He has often been in the front line of negotiations and relations with the European Commission, notably in the run-up to Greece joining the European Monetary Union (EMU). He deals with important ECOFIN matters and shapes the positions to be presented by the Minister, usually enjoying wide discretion in order to provide appropriate and high quality advice. In this he works closely with the EU Directorate.

Relying on a consolidated administrative structure linked to the diplomatic service, the MFA has preserved its lead coordinating role throughout the years. By contrast, the MEA and economic coordination experienced a series of organizational changes. The major part of these changes coincided with the crisis year, albeit having no direct link to the crisis. This is why it is difficult to separate a 'before' and 'after' the crisis in this respect. Leaving aside details, changes for the MEA consisted, for instance, in: a) the merger with sectoral departments, such as trade, industry, tourism, etc., and b) the merger (2001–2002) with, and split (2009) from, the MF.[3]

More important than the short-lived experiments is the underlying criterion for the new arrangements, in particular the separation of finance from economy and economic development issues. Two major consequences result from the successive re-arrangements:

- A wide range of economic sectors and development issues, relevant for internal market policies, the participation in the Council of Competitiveness, and the transposition of corresponding Community Directives into national law, joined the remit of the MEA.
- After the split of the MEA from the MF (2009), the MF retained certain EU policy issues, especially within the Directorate General of Economic Policy (DGEP).

The most eloquent example is the EU Directorate, which prepares ECOFIN and Eurogroup Councils. Furthermore, the SOE was attached to the MF, which also retained the appointment of the economic adviser at the Permanent Representation. Both the SOE and the economic adviser enjoyed the trust of the Minister of Finance. As a result of these changes, domestic economic EU policy coordination came to be shared between the MF and the MEA.

2.2 Governmental coordination

Central Government coordination is generally weak (OECD 2011). The Greek political-administrative culture and patterns of operation tend to defy central and (even more) institutionalized coordination. Several timid attempts at reversing this state of affairs have failed. Informal coordination efforts have to counter departmentalism and political centrifugalism rooted in the political culture. Sectoral rationales tend to resist central coordination and this weakness is often the result of the deficient process of setting priorities and planning their execution.[4]

2.2.1 The PM's role in EU affairs

As the leader of a parliamentary majority endowed with important institutional powers and for political and historical reasons, the PM has been a strong political figure in Greece.[5] However, the necessary staff and services to assist his coordinating role have never developed sufficiently. More specifically, his role in EU policy coordination can be described as minimal and distanced. At most he can inspire a sense of priority and thus mobilize his cabinet in that direction.

Even the former PM Simitis (1996–2004), with doubtless European leanings, did not assume a regular coordinating role, thus leaving the initiative for policy formulation and management to the MFA and, on occasion, to the relevant sectoral ministries. He deliberately omitted to create a special unit for EU affairs, though he closely monitored European policy issues through the Bureau for Strategic Planning and the Diplomatic Bureau. Those matters that risked provoking friction between ministries were brought to his attention, but only if there was some dysfunction in the relationship between the MFA and other ministries. Crisis management and conflict resolution functions are part and parcel of a PM's function and they were dealt with in an informal way. These features continued to characterize the conduct of his successors, in spite of their different approaches towards the collegiality of governmental operation and the varying frequency of governmental meetings.

In terms of support services, a series of incremental changes upgraded the 'Office of the PM' to the 'General Secretariat of the PM' (presidential decree 2/2011) between 2010 and 2012.

A 'Strategic Planning Unit' and an 'EU and International Relations Office' were established, in 2011 and 2012 respectively. The former was to improve oversight in the monitoring of the implementation of governmental work and reforms, in cooperation with responsible ministries. The latter was tasked with analysing European and international developments.

2.2.2 Cabinet and cabinet committees

The General Secretariat of the Government (GSG) is the longstanding supporting structure for governmental coordination; in practice, however, it never really developed to match its requirements. The GSG is headed by the Secretary General, a political appointee, who is in contact with his counterparts in the ministries. Benefiting from the PM's support, he has the potential to mobilize and coordinate, but this occurs with varying frequency[6] and efficiency. Simitis (2005, 469) notes that this form of interministerial coordination was undermined by the personal character of ministerial power, which did not grant the Secretary General enough space to respond to central governmental coordination.

Issues with a European dimension were often discussed at the Council of Ministers (*ypourgikó symvoúlio, υπουργικό συμβούλιο*) (Simitis 2005) or eventually at the Governmental Committee – a body with general competence, in which participation was restricted to selected ministers. However, these discussions seemed to have an informational rather than a decision-making focus (Xiros 2006, 177).

Regarding European policies, the GSG support services were provided with an Office for International and Community Issues in 2010. Its tasks consisted in monitoring European legislation and reporting especially on: a) the transposition of EU law into the Greek legal order, and b) the developments before Community bodies concerning transgressions of EU law by Greek authorities. The creation of this office is linked to the monitoring of compliance with EU legislation,[7] which has significantly improved since 2010.[8]

To conclude, the importance of an institutionalized coordinating body at the political level appears overrated. As Peters (1998, 49–52) suggests, almost any structural device appears potentially workable if there is sufficient political will and managerial desire to make it work. Conversely, no mechanism is sufficient if there is an absence of determination to cooperate. In the case of Greece, specialized governmental EU coordination bodies were short-lived and fell into inertia.[9] Some *ad hoc* specialized committees had a similar fate. The Greek political-administrative culture resists formal, institutionalized, horizontal coordination mechanisms (Spanou 1998, 2000). To put it bluntly, informal processes might just as well do the job to the extent that the political culture is 'coordination-friendly'. Conversely, a 'coordination-averse' culture deeply undermines institutionalized structures.

EU policy coordination efforts have constantly been constrained by various political and cultural factors. On the nine-step policy coordination scale (OECD 1996), the Greek system fares quite low (between 1 and 4). In this context, the negative coordination ambition involves lower transaction costs, since governments may 'trade off' coordination against other important values such as organizational harmony, transparency, flexibility, and accountability (Kassim 2001, 8).

The MFA-led coordination, focused on uploading national positions, has a decentralized – if not fragmented – and a 'bottom-up' character. It thus builds on the preferences of individual ministries rather than around central, 'top-down' priorities, as described by the 'truncated pyramid' metaphor. It operates with a high degree of informality and is mostly *ad hoc*. At best, it tends to rely on personal networks and the capabilities of a small number of people placed in key positions to overcome resistance and weaknesses (Spanou 2000, 2003).

But there is another twist to this narrative. Minimal coordination ambitions are sufficient for uploading the domestic position as long as implementation and enforcement are not priorities. The implementation stage of the EU policy cycle tends to be overlooked by coordinators (Kassim 2001, 11–15). Instead, they focus on the complex, time-consuming policy formulation process that requires bargaining and alliance-building in a context of high institutional fragmentation and sectionalization (Wright 1996, 151–152). There are no immediate sanctions, while any problem can be kicked into the long grass.

Downloading, implementation, and enforcement belong to the national level and need to mobilize a wide array of domestic organizations and activities. They appear even more fragmented, given that the initiative lies with sectoral ministries. It is in that area that priorities changed drastically under the MoU, which the next section outlines.

3 Crisis and adjustments

The two Economic Adjustment Programmes (EAP) agreed upon with the Troika in 2010 and 2012, as well as the third in 2015 agreed upon with the European Commission on behalf of the European Stability Mechanism (ESM)[10] defined a number of policy priorities. They aimed at economic, fiscal, legal, and social adjustments, and included an unprecedented number and level of compliance requirements in order to tackle sovereign indebtedness and reduce the risk of international systemic spill-over. Sets of 'prior actions' had to be fulfilled under extreme time pressure because the continuation of financial assistance to Greece was conditional on the Troika's quarterly review missions.

The EAP and the accompanying MoU shaped a new policy environment in Greece, namely policy conditionality. This restricted the freedom of government actors in their decision-making, yet it also meant opportunities to promote fiscal consolidation measures and urgently needed structural reforms, but also risks associated with the (non-)implementation of compliance requirements.

Conditionality became the central policy instrument (Lascoumes and Le Galès 2007) of the EAP. Far from being technical, it had important implications for the re-shaping of domestic governance and the coordination of EU policy. Conditionality has provided a new policy narrative to frame problems and solutions through the lens of the emergency situation and the risks involved. It combined MoU obligations with financial (and technical) assistance and techniques for monitoring results. Conditionality has contributed to the structuring of a new policy environment. The main question is therefore how the political-administrative system in Greece reacted to these new conditions.

3.1 MoU: policies and actors

Beyond the immediate need for fiscal consolidation, the sovereign debt crisis was framed as a competitiveness problem that required internal devaluation, market liberalization, and labour-market reforms. The MoU(s) defined:

- *Policy priorities*, a large part of which was (and is) linked to EU policies;
- *New institutional actors* interacting with the domestic political administrative system to monitor and support implementation.

3.1.1 New priorities

While the first MoU focused on short-term fiscal consolidation, it also comprised an ambitious structural reform agenda to strengthen external competitiveness, accelerate the reallocation of resources from the non-tradable to the tradable sector, and foster growth. It included reforms

> to modernize the public sector, to render product and labour markets more efficient and flexible, and create a more open and accessible business environment for domestic and foreign investors, including a reduction of the State's direct participation in domestic industries.
>
> (*European Economy* 2010, 10)

Considering that Greece lagged behind in the implementation of key EU directives in the area of services, energy, and transport, most required reforms concerned the internal market and affected a large number of economic and financial interests. For instance, the (liberalization of the) Services Directive[11] required the introduction of horizontal as well as sector-specific legislation in priority areas (e.g. tourism, education, and retail), while regulated professions and network industries (transport, energy) were to be liberalized (*ibid.* 22–23, 49), and the role and independence of regulatory authorities were to be strengthened in line with EU policies. Last but not least, the programme involved the necessary improvement of the absorption rate of EU structural and cohesion funds.

While preserving the priorities of the first MoU, the second one covered an even larger span of policy areas and a larger number of EU directives.[12] It is worth noting that a significant part of these directives included more recent ones (2009 and later). The imposed conditionality of the MoU accelerated the transposition of the directives – even ahead of their deadlines. The third

MoU (August 2015) was similar in this regard.[13] This points to a kind of 'forced' Europeanization that used pre-existing solutions and tools to tackle a sovereign debt crisis framed predominantly as an economic competitiveness problem.

In sum, the MoU brought about an opportunity to advance certain European economic policies that involve the transposition and/or effective implementation of a series of EU directives as a means to achieve them.[14] Thus, conditionality provided the link between the MoU requirements and the domestic EU policy coordination system.

3.1.2 New actors: the representatives of the international creditors

A new network of organizations linked to the MoU requirements emerged in Greece. The Troika (and since August 2015 the 'Quartet') set the pace, calendar, and priorities of domestic policy compliance on the basis of quarterly 'evaluation' or (joint) 'review' missions and thus evaluate whether the prerequisites were fulfilled for the disbursement of the next tranche of the loan agreement.[15] The Troika standard operation procedure relied on on-site representatives who worked closely with the various ministries, monitoring the implementation of measures and the achievement of targets. A representation office of the IMF settled in Athens to monitor policy in mid-2010.

Furthermore, in mid-2011 a Task Force for Greece (TFGR)[16] was established by the European Commission – upon the request of the Greek Government. It represented, in close cooperation with the authorities, an innovative form of EU presence that monitored of compliance with the economic adjustment programme, following policy development and providing technical assistance in order to meet the terms of the adjustment programme. It also assisted the authorities with taking measures for an accelerated absorption of EU funds, focusing on competitiveness, growth, and employment. To achieve these objectives, it was decided to ensure an appropriate operational presence with two teams; one in Brussels and one in Athens (until early 2015).[17]

The programme of technical assistance coordinated by the TFGR was quite extensive. It covered thirteen broad policy fields, each comprising a number of sub-projects. Some members of the TFGR were embedded in individual ministries, e.g. the MF for purposes of tax-revenue compliance. Its staff held regular bilateral discussions with the various responsible ministries. The TFGR eventually operated as a mediator between Greek authorities (ministries, PM services, etc.) and institutional stakeholders (interest organizations, e.g. the Union of Greek Banks) to promote specific policy priorities, sometimes compensating for the domestic lack of coordination, mobilization, and problem-solving capacity.

The TFGR's direct access to the Commission combined with local knowledge, especially in the Athens-based team, prepared or facilitated negotiations and agreements with the Commission services on issues such as the acceleration of the use of Community funds.[18] However, this role was to remain discreet and in the shadow of the more neutral mission of providing and coordinating technical assistance.

The importance of these new institutional actors relates to the constant presence of foreign technocrats monitoring the implementation of the MoU either in the capacity of technical assistance for pre-agreed reform roadmaps or in the capacity of on-going progress evaluation. These local teams were in regular contact with the relevant Greek ministries at the administrative as well as the political level. Their presence put pressure on the Greek political administrative system 'to deliver' and 'do its homework'. These new actors were deeply involved in micromanaging reforms while focusing on numeric targets and Excel-sheets box ticking.

The local teams tended to become part of the crisis-related domestic administrative machinery. The instrumentation of MoU policies (see Lascoumes and Le Galès 2007; Kassim and Le Galès 2010) reflected a power relation difficult to dissimulate, despite the use of technical terms such as 'monitoring', 'evaluation', or 'technical assistance'. The recurring pictures of the Troika's visits to various ministries became the media's narrative of an asymmetrical relationship. In a symbolic move, the SYRIZA-led Government, elected in January 2015, constructed a different arrangement. It rejected the term Troika and created different levels of negotiations with the creditors: the Athens group (technical level) and the Brussels group (mission-chief level with government representatives) next to the Ministers of Finance meetings and the PM's meetings with his counterparts.

3.2 Coordinating the implementation of the MoU and EU policies

This *modus operandi* unleashed increased pressure for coordination and cooperation between domestic actors and organizations. The need for coordination was driven by, among other important factors, financial constraints, cross-cutting issues, the international dimension of policy, and membership in supranational organizations (Peters 1998, 10–12). All of these are present in the MoU.

3.2.1 Coordination pressures

The extensive list of 'prior actions' to be implemented confronted the Greek political-administrative system with a complex problem: it could not be fulfilled by just one ministry nor could it be handled by a single organization because the actions cut across most public organizations and policies. It can therefore be described as a 'wicked issue' (Christensen et al. 2015), the tackling of which required new, overarching coordination capacity to overcome resistance, delays, sectoral interests, and the general inertia of sectoral administrations.

A better central coordination would prove essential for the political-administrative system in Greece to respond to these requirements. The pressing priorities of the MoU could not be satisfied with the 'bottom-up', decentralized, negative coordination practices (described in the previous section) with regard to the uploading of national positions in Brussels. Some degree of positive coordination involved a sustained effort by political and administrative actors to ensure compliance with the demanded priorities, timetables, and stringent conditions, as well as to ensure tighter controls over the activity of various public organizations.

In general, governments facing crises tend to strengthen central authority and steering. Coordination practices aimed at increasing prospective efficiency tend to be top-down, hierarchical,[19] politically centred, and tend to lean towards imposition rather than towards bargaining in order to lower transaction costs, and minimize conflict and competition in the public sector. In Greece, the high number of 'prior actions' and the clear sanctions for failing to fulfil them triggered a shift towards centralized decision-making (Peters 1998, 16–19). However, the weakness of coordination in the Greek 'centre of government' and the need to 'take account of the EU legislative dimension' had been emphatically underlined by the Organisation for Economic Cooperation and Development (OECD) following a functional review report by the central administration.[20]

Central coordination adjusted very slowly and marginally to the challenge. For a long time, no specialized governmental structures for the coordination of the MoU implementation were established. The cabinet and its standing committees would eventually deal with various policy aspects according to their existing competencies. A deputy PM had the oversight with a coordinating, yet in practice, secondary role.

On the contrary, the MF's involvement in EU issues, even after the outbreak of the crisis, remained stable due to its participation in the Eurogroup and Euroworking Group. These intergovernmental bodies are autonomous from the rest of the EU apparatus. The Minister of Finance and the President of the SOE became the new centre for the management of the crisis and the coordination of MoU implementation. They remained in close and direct communication with the PM, who, nevertheless, preserved a role of last resort, mostly backing the MF vis-à-vis other ministries.

3.2.2 Political centralization

The new policy environment triggered *de facto* adjustments. It induced political centralization of decisions: most of the important issues were discussed between the Minister of Finance, the President of the SOE, and the PM. The high stakes of decision-making in order to access the next loan tranche and the conditions under which financial assistance would be provided led to policy centralization within a small core of participants. This practice reached its peak during the (re-)negotiation of the MoU in the first semester of 2015. The PM further undertook systematic bilateral contacts with their counterparts (especially those from Germany and France). Centralization and bilateral informal contacts have become a constant feature of dealing with MoU requirements. Other current high-profile issues (such as the relocation of refugees) seem to follow the same pattern.

An indicator of this centralization is that the issues were not discussed substantively at the Council of Ministers, despite regular meetings. There was neither collective preparation nor formulation according to ministerial competence. Agreements tended to be managed solely by the three main actors (PM, President of the SOE, Minister of Finance). Their decisions were later presented at the Council of Ministers to be approved, with the aim of involving all ministers in the political responsibility for their implementation. This *modus operandi* is directly related to the restrictions imposed on the freedom of decision-making and the compliance requirements in the MoU.

Only marginal adjustments took place under these conditions. Interministerial committees were formed on an *ad hoc* basis for the preparation of specific issues, e.g. when the Government wanted to present an alternative measure to those recommended by the Troika. For instance, such committees were formed with regard to a tax exemption for (hybrid) environmentally friendly cars and measures for indebted households.

Political centralization reached a point where institutionalized mechanisms were marginalized. For instance, in the initial stages of the crisis, the Minister of Finance sometimes bypassed the MFA and the Permanent Representative and cooperated directly with the economic adviser (based at the Permanent Representation), who accompanied the Troika in its evaluation missions, attended the meetings, and was in regular contact with the SOE. Personal networks helped to overcome such gaps in cooperation and communication.

Cooperation between the President of the SOE, the PM, and the Minister of Finance proved crucial for the fulfilment of the MoU. However, the quality of cooperation varied due to political affinity (in coalition governments from 2011 onwards) or the personal chemistry between the relevant personalities. This centralized coordination scheme would also set the priorities for the promotion of European policies.

3.2.3 Improving central coordination

A new instance of general coordination was established[21] following a requirement of the MoU as well as OECD and TFGR recommendations: the General Secretariat for Coordination, which is attached to the PM and headed by a political appointee (law 4109/2013); however, it is not fully operational yet. The description of its tasks does not explicitly mention MoU monitoring, coordination, or European policies; it refers more generally to efficient policy coordination and consistent organization, implementation, and monitoring of governmental work, which includes dealing with disagreements between members of the Government, and a conflict resolution mechanism for joint or overlapping competences.

Some of these institutional changes to improve general policy coordination may be linked to an increased need to deal with the monitoring of MoU requirements. In this respect, these changes eventually necessitated reforming EU policy coordination. However, despite the volume of EU policies and directives involved in the implementation of the MoU, no major changes to the existing EU policy coordination system have emerged.

3.2.4 The MF as the focal point

Despite the overall political responsibility of the PM, the hub of the new coordination challenges was placed elsewhere. The instrument of conditionality favoured not only centralization but also a specific locus: the MF, which co-signed the MoU. This Ministry was the first to gain awareness of the stakes involved: being spared economic sanctions (e.g. sovereign default) constituted the main reward for strict compliance. The MF's leading role in dealing with the crisis and as the main interlocutor of the Eurogroup and the Troika for financial assistance and economic adjustment strengthened its status vis-à-vis other line ministries.

Beyond fiscal consolidation, the MF came to bear the general responsibility for the state of the economy and was the focal point for monitoring and coordinating the implementation of the MoU (*European Economy* 2010, 90). It had the contacts with the Troika and the Eurozone members and therefore a clear view of priorities as to what was to be done domestically. In any case, there was no other body capable of, or willing to take on, this responsibility. The MF became the centre of gravity for political and administrative influence. In the words of a public official involved, it had to be 'ten steps ahead of other ministries'.[22]

In this role, the General Secretariat of Fiscal Policy (General Accounting Office) was crucial. It was part of the monitoring mechanism within the MF and covered a wide range of fiscal areas (State budget and expenditure, public debt, State guarantees for loan agreements, salary scales for civil servants, and

State pensions). The Ministry's monitoring responsibility for the entire programme also included the oversight of 'structural reforms' in collaboration with several other ministries.

The Secretary General of the MF ensured the (informal) coordination of his counterparts in other involved ministries by holding systematic information meetings. In its monitoring role for the MoU, the MF further relied on the SOE, the General Secretariat of Economic Policy, and, more specifically, its EU Directorate. The SOE came to be less of a think tank and more of an actor involved in the everyday management of European economic policy issues.[23] In the new policy environment, without any formal changes, the SOE assumed a leading role. The staff remained small (currently, six out of ten positions are filled) and the role of the council members constrained. In spite of this limited bureaucratic arrangement, its President is the substitute for the Minister of Finance in the Eurogroup and ECOFIN and the representative of the country at the Euro Working Group and the European Financial Committee. He has also represented the PM at EU summit conferences.

Actions and measures that were discussed at sectoral level with the technical staff of the Troika were submitted to the MF. The Minister (or Junior Minister) of Finance and the President of the SOE presented and discussed them with the PM. Then, they were presented to the Council of Ministers so that members of the Government prepared to implement them. With the support of the PM, the MF would ensure coordination of the implementation of the MoU by putting pressure on sectoral ministries.

The monitoring and coordinating of the first MoU relied on SOE staff, who were following the activity of various ministries, however, this changed over time. The second MoU contained even more detailed requirements for structural reform, including roadmaps and timetables that needed a much closer ('line to line') monitoring. The volume of work clearly exceeded the capacity of the limited staff of the SOE.

The Troika requested a specialized structure with permanent (non-politically appointed) staff to ensure continuity in delivering the supporting work. Law 4002/2011 (Article 23) provided for a formal monitoring mechanism for the structural adjustment programme, which was also mentioned in the second MoU (*European Economy* 2012, 165). It was only in 2013, however, that the Service for the Planning and Monitoring of the Implementation of Economic Adjustment Programmes, directly attached to the Minister of Finance, became operational.[24] Its purpose was to assist the political leadership in the planning, implementation, monitoring, evaluation, and updating of fiscal and structural action plans.[25]

This Service's competence extends to all ministries. It cooperates with the SOE for the formulation of measures and for their implementation, and assists agencies involved in the negotiations and the representation of the country in European (and international) organizations. In light of the quarterly reports, it collects data on implementation and progress assessment. When MoU requirements involve compliance with European legislation, it also cooperates with the EU Directorate of the MF. The change in the Government in January 2015 and the increased political centralization stemming from the high-level (re-)negotiation of the MoU in the first semester of that year rather sidelined the operational services.

In sum, the absence of any consolidated governmental coordination body turned the MF into the focal point for the monitoring and coordination of sectoral ministries that are required to reduce costs and implement reforms. Remedying the generally weak coordination capacity of the political-administrative system involves power resources that the MF has from its traditional role, more than any core government structure. Fiscal discipline as the prime MoU obligation has consolidated its influence over other ministries.

These reasons partly explain organizational developments in functional terms, i.e. as stemming from new needs and requirements linked to the MoU. However, one may also detect a deeper transformation: the MF has become the bridge into the Greek political-administrative system for the adoption of selected policies while sidelining other domestic institutions and actors (MFA, sectoral ministries, but also Parliament).

4 Impact on the EU coordination system

The new policy conditions shaped by MoU conditionality did not trigger significant institutional adjustment in terms of specialized EU coordination structures. However, informal and/or *ad hoc* mechanisms were developed to deal with the new issues and challenges. The major impact of the new policy environment is expressed by the *de facto* rise of the MF as the lead ministry and the selective prioritization of EU policies.

4.1 Readjustments due to the MoU

The domestic EU policy coordination system is mainly geared towards participation in EU policy formation and the uploading of national positions. It exhibits a limited concern to follow transposition and implementation, this part being mainly the responsibility of sectoral departments. From this point of view, the MFA-led decentralized and negative coordination scheme has hardly been affected. In contrast, the MoU-related emphasis on downloading selected directives brought to the fore the coordinating role of the MF.

4.2 Emphasis on downloading and the MF

The actions and policies included in the MoU focused on swift compliance with relevant EU legislation. Having the responsibility for the implementation of the MoU, the MF became more interventionist regarding structural reforms for issues that normally fall within the competence of other ministries (e.g. the internal market, the opening of regulated professions, labour market liberalization, etc.). As mentioned above, these required the 'downloading' (transposition) and implementation of a series of EU directives. No other structure had a comprehensive responsibility for the implementation of EU policies; therefore, the MF came to be involved in the domestic coordination of EU policies and acted as the driving force to overcome potential resistance.[26]

The actual implementation of policies faced challenges. The liberalization of services, for example, touched upon numerous people employed: in transport, open markets (fresh products), taxi drivers, lawyers, pharmacists, etc. The new role of the MF involving the oversight of policy implementation was not readily accepted by the network of sectoral ministries that were exposed to the discontent of corresponding interest groups. Though already a powerful institutional actor, the MF often had to rely on the backing and intervention of the PM.

There has been a longstanding debate concerning the mode of incorporation of European directives, i.e. whether the incorporation should occur by law or presidential decree. For many years, the latter had been seen as a more convenient and flexible tool for the Government, which, however, implied the exclusion of parliamentary debate on the relevant issues. Under the MoU, the incorporation of European directives mostly took place by law. Debate was again limited due to the urgency procedures used, the volume and heterogeneity of items in the (omnibus) bills, and the lack of time.

4.3 Uploading national positions: business as usual?

The MFA-led uploading coordination survived in parallel and continued its routine operation around the same structures, processes, and difficulties. The two-level approach, i.e. EU and Eurozone, set the scene for a new division of labour. Issues discussed at the Eurogroup of Finance Ministers remain under the exclusive responsibility of the MF. Therefore, the greater the volume of Eurozone requirements, the less the involvement of other ministries, particularly the MFA.

Regarding economic coordination more generally, the MFA is informed about issues that have to be discussed at the COREPER II. ECOFIN issues are prepared by the EU Directorate of the MF under the authority of the President of the SOE. The Permanent Representative is informed and accompanies the Minister of Finance (or the President of the SOE). The MFA hardly has any involvement in this process. If issues discussed at the Eurogroup later go to the ECOFIN, the EU Directorate of the MF cooperates with MFA services with a view to transferring the national positions to the Permanent Representation. These positions are most often sent at the last moment and relayed to both the MFA and the Permanent Representation in order to take into account the latest developments in the working groups.

Not surprisingly, the MF actively follows ECOFIN discussions and developments regarding the 'new economic governance'.[27] The MF became additionally involved in EU policy formation, i.e. the shaping of national positions in MoU priority areas such as intersectoral issues of the single market. The participation in the Council of Competitiveness is shared between the MF (Directorate for EU) and the MEA (sectoral issues). Contrary to implementation (downloading), cooperation with other ministries for the preparation of national positions (uploading) seems to be smoother, possibly because of the aforementioned features of the EU decision-making process.

Pushing for further structural reform seems to account for this increased involvement of the MF in the uploading of national positions regarding the internal market. The risk that sectoral ministries may be less effective because they are more vulnerable to the pressure of interest groups might further explain this 'duplication' in selected areas of EU policy formation.

As a secondary effect of the need to comply with MoU-relevant EU requirements, the capacity to participate in the EU policy-formation process has improved. Catching up in sectors where the country used to appear as a laggard in transposing and implementing EU legislation seems to have strengthened the country's stance within the EU. All this provides an impulse for more active participation in the EU policy process regarding reforms that are relevant for the single market, such as the proposed 'deepening [of] the Services Directive' and the promotion of 'its ambitious implementation'.

More generally, the MF established its presence in areas of this new policy environment that were beyond its core activities. Starting with the Eurozone membership and despite (or thanks to!) the 2009 split, the MF strengthened its oversight of the Greek economy, going beyond fiscal issues. This was further consolidated when it assumed the central responsibility for monitoring and implementing the MoU. To a large extent, the MF has replaced the MEA in domestic EU-related economic coordination, depriving it of a part of its mission. The latter retained responsibility for structural funds but no longer has the resources to ensure the wider economic coordination.

The MF further developed a higher coordination ambition with regard to its responsibility for MoU implementation. A centralized, positive, and selective coordination system centred around a domestically powerful institutional actor is opposed to the MFA-led, decentralized, negative coordination scheme. The latter corresponds to a 'hybrid' structure to the extent that it operates within a (vertically structured) network of other ministries regarding its coordinating and supervisory functions (Christensen et al. 2015, 5). On the scale of policy coordination, the MF-led coordination scheme selectively moved towards steps seven and eight (OECD 1996). Rather than arbitrating organizational differences (step six), the MF has the role of a central organization 'setting parameters on the discretion of individual organizations' and 'establishing government priorities', i.e. MoU requirements. From 'decentralized and selective', the EU coordination system developed around the MF changed into 'centralized and selective' in both the ascending and the descending phases of decision-making processes related to the MoU requirements.

4.4 MoU and EU policy implementation: two different facets

The conditions for the implementation of the MoU reveal the critical differences between the new policy environment on the one hand and usual EU procedures on the other. The latter take time and provide the opportunity to debate, form coalitions, and influence the outcome. In contrast, through the MoU the Troika used time and political pressure on the Government to deliver on predefined reforms with the expectation of immediate results. These institutional and political constraints explain the gradual development of the MoU's own monitoring and coordination mechanisms, albeit with minimal contact with the EU policy-coordination system.

Furthermore, the MoU prioritized certain EU policies over others. For instance, when obligations stemming from the Memorandum entered into conflict with European (procedural or substantial) rules, the latter took a back seat. Rarely would the Troika accept an argument that their recommendations contravened EU regulation and therefore could not proceed. To illustrate, the tight deadlines imposed by the MoU for public tender procedures made it impossible to respect relevant EU standards and obligations; issues important for the EU but not for the IMF were ignored.

Labour market policies typically reflect this divergence. Collective labour relations have been deconstructed without consultation with the social partners (Papadimitriou 2012). Achtsioglou and Doherty (2014) underline the 'micro-management by the Troika concerning labour market regulation' and highlight the incompatibility of the required reforms with the principles of the EU social model, particularly policies to respect and enhance social dialogue and the collective autonomy of social partners.[28]

More generally, Parliament could in practice only sanction decisions already taken by the executive, many of which imposed limitations on fundamental and social rights.[29] Consultation with civil society stakeholders became virtually impossible. To speed up the process and avoid painful confrontations, successive governments repeatedly resorted to the rule of party discipline when voting on bills, the urgency procedures curtailing parliamentary discussions (Article 76 of the constitution) and executive orders (acts of legislative content); with the latter, they by-passed Parliament, which, according to the constitution, only had to approve the executive orders *ex post*.

The European Commission performed a double role: first, as a member of the Troika next to the European Central Bank; second, as the focus of the EU legislative and monitoring mechanism. In the 'grey zone of ambivalence' (Contiades and Tassopoulos 2013, 202), the paradox of a split appeared: the Commission within the Troika and the (rest of the) Commission outside the Troika demanded that Greece fulfil the various requirements which were sometimes contradictory and certainly reflected different priorities. Transgressing European legislation was a non-issue for the Commission within the Troika; thus, there is a different EU for programme countries.

5 Conclusion

The post-2009 crisis management in Greece led to the MoU and the shaping of a new policy environment. The MF gained a central place in the EU policy-coordination system through the novel policy instrument of conditionality in particular. Beyond fiscal consolidation, compliance requirements led to a different prioritization of EU issues, depending on their relevance for the MoU. This 'forced Europeanization' further provided a substitute for a referential framework, the missing link of the governmental steering described as the 'truncated pyramid' (Spanou 2000, 178).

A separate 'emergency' mechanism was built for the monitoring and coordination of MoU implementation. To the extent that its requirements included EU policies, the centre of gravity moved away from the MFA and towards the MF. The latter had the upper hand in imposing MoU-related priorities regarding European policy issues. The push for pro-active participation in the EU policy process is a side-effect of the acceleration of EU-policy-related reforms under MoU conditionality. But this also revolves around the MF, which is now more involved in the process of shaping and uploading national positions for selected intersectoral policies (e.g. the single market).

EU legislation was sidelined when it conflicted with MoU requirements and deadlines. This asymmetry became evident when European regulations were seen as obstacles to procedural requirements and to actions that needed to be taken within extremely tight deadlines. It further confirmed a parallel asymmetry that resulted from the systematic lack of respect for parliamentary procedures, which accounts for the democratic deficit imposed by MoU deadlines and 'prior action' obligations.

From a new-institutionalist perspective, the coordination system adjusted within the existing State capacities and institutional legacies in an *ad hoc*, gradual, and basically informal manner, with minor interventions in formal structures. The emergence or re-adjustment of coordination arrangements followed the pre-existing patterns of response typical of the Greek political-administrative system.

Confirming historical and cultural institutional perspectives, adjustment occurred slowly and started with *ad hoc* practices and an emphasis on personal relationships, and later developed rather slim coordination structures around the MF. The MoU coordination system was juxtaposed to, or rather super-imposed on, the EU policy coordination system. It did not alter existing arrangements but rather added new institutional elements to existing ones, creating a process of institutional layering (Streeck and Thelen 2005).

Crises are frequently seen as potential 'critical junctures' in the sense of 'moments when substantial institutional change takes place thereby creating a "branching point" from which historical development moves onto a new path' (Hall and Taylor 1996, 942). For the domestic EU policy-coordination system, the experience of the economic crisis does not seem to have been such a critical juncture. No substantial change can be detected in the MFA-led network.

However, incremental adjustments rather than a radical shift characterize the displacement of the locus for economic coordination of EU policies. In the Greek political-administrative context, the MF had the necessary resources for this role more than any other institution of the central Government. It is unclear how deep these changes are. Greece remains in troubled waters and the implementation of the third Memorandum only started in the autumn of 2015.

Nevertheless, these changes cannot be seen in isolation. They are partly due to a more general shift in the perception of EU policy priorities and integration perspectives at the European level. Another aspect of the institutionalist perspective thus comes to the fore: the link between institutional structures and the perceptions that become influential at certain points in time. This broader shift has favoured the displacement of economic coordination towards the MF and legitimized the extension of its involvement in selected EU policies beyond its core tasks. More specifically, the centrality of the MF in economic policy coordination vis-à-vis the EU (and the creditor institutions) is in line with the Fiscal Compact and the new economic governance model; this puts the emphasis on the primacy of economy and competition over social policies and fiscal space as well as on the increased monitoring and oversight authority of the Commission and the DG for Economic and Financial Affairs (ECFIN) in particular. Thus, the star of all

Finance Ministries is rising, a trend that appears more clearly in the framework devised for programme countries.

Notes

1 This is the former Ministry of Coordination, which lost its (outwardly) leading role to the Ministry of Foreign Affairs in the years after accession (see: Spanou 2000, 166 ff).

2 The SOE is composed of: a Scientific Council, which forms a 'think-tank' comprising seven academics chosen by the Minister for a three-year term; an Economic Research and Analysis Unit, staffed by a maximum of 10 experts on contract; and a Secretariat.

3 Due to space constraints, only some relevant changes are presented here. Successive re-organizations created the Ministry of Development (1996), of Economy, Competitiveness and Shipping (2009), and of Development and Competitiveness (2013) as well as the super-Ministry of Economy, Merchant Marine and Tourism (January 2015) and of Economy, Development and Tourism (September 2015). The internal structure of the merged ministries was left intact.

4 This is an expression of a deeper phenomenon summarized as the weak steering capacity of the Greek State (Spanou 1996 and 2000, 176).

5 Single-party Government was the rule in Greek politics until 2011, which used to endow the PM with non-negligible political weight. The PM directs and coordinates the activities of the Government, controls the agenda of the Council of Ministers, and arbitrates in conflicts.

6 The Secretary General meets with his counterparts from other ministries twice a year for approximately two hours, usually to discuss with them the most pressing horizontal policy issues (OECD 2011, 30).

7 In spite of this task, it partly duplicates the long-standing service and activity in legal harmonization with EU legislation of the ENY (MFA).

8 See: http://ec.europa.eu/internal_market/scoreboard/performance_by_member_state/greece/index_en.htm.

9 E.g. the interministerial Committee for the Coordination of Greece-EU Relations set up in 1993 (Spanou 2003).

10 The new coalition Government of PM A. Tsipras (SYRIZA-ANEL) that took office after the 25 January 2015 elections sought to fundamentally renegotiate the second macro-economic adjustment programme. It organized a referendum on the terms of the programme in July 2015. Despite winning the referendum (61:31 per cent), it accepted the third programme in August 2015. It then called early elections in September 2015, which confirmed its coalition majority. The third three-year programme and MoU was agreed upon with the European Commission acting on behalf of the European Stability Mechanism. See: http://ec.europa.eu/economy_finance/assistance_eu_ms/greek_loan_facility/index_en.htm.

11 Laws that transpose the Services Directive 2006/123/EC include law 3844/2010, law 3919/2011, etc. Other directives concerned: Public Procurement (2007/66/EC and 2009/81/EC), Professional Qualifications

(2005/36/EC), and the Better Regulation Agenda, involving a 20 per cent reduction of the administrative burden compared with the 2008 level.

12 Such directives included: Directives 2009/72 and 2009/73/EC (electricity and natural gas); Renewable Energy Directive (2009/28/EC); Council Directive 2009/119/EC (stocks of crude oil and petroleum products); railways directives; Directives 2009/140/EC and 2009/136/EC on electronic communications; Collateral Directive 2002/47/EC; Council Directive 89/105/EEC, the so-called 'Transparency Directive' (prices of medicinal products); and Directive 2003/41/EC on occupational pensions, the Institutions for Occupational Retirement Provision (IORP) Directive.

13 The third MoU involves EU directives issued in 2014 (public procurement and concessions) as well as an action plan to meet the requirements of the Late Payment Directive 2011/7 (laws 4152/2013 and 4254/2014) and the 2012/27 Directive on energy efficiency (which was transposed by law 4342/2015).

14 All the directives mentioned in the first and second MoU have been transposed in time, with the exception of one, 2002/47/EC. This one was included more recently in law 4335/2015 as a precondition for the third MoU. One is still pending (89/105/EEC). See http://www.ggk.gov.gr/?p=3265.

15 See: http://ec.europa.eu/economy_finance/assistance_eu_ms/greek_loan_facility/index_en.htm.

16 Initially attached to the President of the Commission and later to the DG ECFIN See: http://ec.europa.eu/commission_2010-2014/president/pdf/qr6_en.pdf.

17 The TFGR was phased out by June 2015 because the Government elected in January 2015 did not see its necessity. In July 2015, the Commission set up 'a new dedicated Structural Reform Support Service' in Brussels 'to help with the design and monitoring of reforms'. The agreement on a new European Stability Mechanism (ESM) programme for Greece provided for technical assistance. This new technical assistance programme was agreed between the Greek authorities and the European Commission in October 2015. Under the third MoU, all technical assistance financed from European sources is coordinated by the Structural Reform Support Service (SRSS). See: http://ec.europa.eu/economy_finance/assistance_eu_ms/greek_loan_facility/pdf/plan-tc-fin_en.pdf).

18 A lower national co-financing rate was agreed in 2011. By the end of 2014, Greece had spectacularly improved its absorption of EU funds, reaching a ratio of 87,97 per cent and thereby improving its position from eighteenth to third in the EU.

19 As opposed to markets and networks, completing the usual typology of coordinating mechanisms.

20 The report was a requirement of the first MoU (OECD 2011, 30). Its recommendations formed the basis for administrative reforms as part of required structural reforms included in the second MoU.

21 See law 4046/2012 (Annex V_2_ΑΓΓ).

22 It is significant that the law-drafting committee was set up on the initiative of the Minister of Finance for the liberalization of the regulated professions.

23 In the September 2015 Government, the new alternate Minister of Finance retained his role as President of the SOE.

24 After the recent restructuring of the MF (2014), it was renamed 'Operational Planning Unit' and attached to the General Secretariat (GS) of Economic Policy.

25 It also assists with the elaboration of the Growth and Stability Programme(s) and National Reform Programmes by providing relevant information to the responsible services.

26 This entailed passing bills, setting up law-drafting committees, and demanding studies concerning the economic impact of liberalization of services, indicators for liberalization of professions, etc., with the assistance of the TFGR, etc. (see: *European Economy* 2014, 58).

27 The ('six pack') Council Directive 2011/85/EU and the Decision of the European Council of 25 March 2011 on the European Stability Mechanism were transposed by laws 4270/2014 and 4063/2012, respectively.

28 See: Keith Ewing 29 September 2012: http://www.ier.org.uk/news/troika-imposing-illegal-terms-greece. The ILO (2011) had also voiced similar concerns. See: http://www.ilo.org/wcmsp5/groups/public/@ed_norm/@normes/documents/missionreport/wcms_170433.pdf.

29 It is worth noting that the Special Standing Committee on European Affairs seems to have continued the discussion on EU legislation initiatives intensively between 2010 and 2013, with at least two meetings a month. In 2014, the frequency dropped to once a month or less, and very few discussions on EU legislative initiatives took place. 2015 was the year with the fewest meetings of the European Affairs Committee (eight in total). The agenda mostly had to do with updating the Committee on EU developments, but there was no discussion of specific EU directives or regulations. By May 2016, the Committee met just once or twice a month to discuss the refugee crisis and more general issues, such as the institutional developments in the EU and the role of national parliaments, the European economic governance, the participation of the European Parliament in the monitoring of the Greek adjustment programme, etc.

Bibliography

Achtsioglou E. and Doherty M. (2014) 'There Must Be Some Way Out of Here: The Crisis, Labour Rights and Member States in the Eye of the Storm', *European Law Journal* 20 (2) March 2014 (219–240).

Christensen T., Danielsen O.A., Laegreid P. and Rykkja L.H. (2015) 'Comparing Coordination Structures for Crisis Management in Six Countries', *Public Administration* (First published online: 6 July 2015, DOI: 10.1111/padm.12186) (1–17).

Contiades X. and Tassopoulos I.A. (2013) 'The Impact of the Financial Crisis on the Greek Constitution', in Contiades X. (ed.), *Constitutions in the Global Financial Crisis. A Comparative Analysis*, Farnham, Ashgate (195–217).

Dimitrova A. and Toshkov D. (2007) 'The Dynamics of Domestic Coordination of EU Policy in the New Member States: Impossible to Lock In?', *West European Politics* 30 (5) (961–986).

European Economy Occasional Papers (2014) 192; (2012) 94; (2010) 61.
Hall P.A. and Taylor R.C.R. (1996) 'Political Science and the Three New Institutionalisms', *Political Studies* XLIV (936–957).
Ioakimidis P.C. (1993) 'Greek Administration and European Policy Formation', in Tsoukalis L. (ed.), *Greece in the EC. The Challenge of Adjustment*, Athens, EKEM/Papazissis (209–230) [in Greek].
Kassim H. (2001) 'Introduction', in Kassim H., Menon A., Peters B.G. and Wright V. (eds.), *The National Coordination of EU Policy: The European Level*, Oxford, Oxford University Press (1–46).
Kassim H. and Le Galès P. (2010) 'Exploring Governance in a Multi-Level Polity: A Policy Instruments Approach', *West European Politics* 33 (1) (1–21).
Laegreid P., Randma-Liiv T., Rykkja L.H. and Sarapuu K. (2015) 'Emerging Coordination Practices of European Central Governments', *International Review of Administrative Sciences* 81 (2) (346–351).
Lascoumes P. and Le Galès P. (2007) 'Introduction: Understanding Public Policy through its Instruments. From the Nature of Instruments to the Sociology of Public Policy Instrumentation', *Governance* 20 (1) (1–21).
OECD (1996) *Globalisation: What Challenges and Opportunities for Governments?*, Paris, OECD/GD (96) 64.
OECD (2011) *Greece. Review of the Central Administration*, Paris, OECD Public Governance Reviews.
Papadimitriou C. (2012) 'Le droit du travail grec face à la crise. Un passage dangereux vers une nouvelle physionomie juridique', *Revue de Droit Comparé du Travail et de la Sécurité Sociale* IV (2) (6–16).
Passas A. and Petraki E. (2009) 'The Greek Administration in the EU Political Process', in Passas A. and Tsekos Th.N. (eds.), *National Administration and European Integration*, Athens, Papazissis (143–197) [in Greek].
Peters B.G. (1998) *Managing Horizontal Government. The Politics of Coordination*, Canadian Centre for Management Development, Research paper n. 21.
Simitis K. (2005) *Policies for a Creative Greece*, Athens, Polis [in Greek].
Spanou C. (1996) 'On the Regulatory Capacity of the Hellenic State', *International Review of Administrative Sciences* 62 (2) (219–237).
Spanou C. (1998) 'European Integration in Administrative Terms. A Framework for Analysis and the Greek Case', *Journal of European Public Policy* 5 (3) (467–840).
Spanou C. (2000) 'A Truncated Pyramid? Domestic Coordination of EU Policy in Greece', in Kassim H., Peters B.G. and Wright V. (eds.), *The National Co-ordination of EU Policy: The Domestic Level*, Oxford, Oxford University Press (161–181).
Spanou C. (2001) 'Permanent Challenges? Representing Greece in Brussels', in Kassim H., Menon A., Peters B.G. and Wright V. (eds.), *The National Co-ordination of EU Policy: The European Level*, Oxford, Oxford University Press (147–167).
Spanou C. (2003) 'Managing Europe from Home. The Europeanization of the Greek Core Executive', *Organizing for EU Enlargement*. Occasional papers no 4.1 09 03 (5th Framework Programme) www.oeue.net.

Streeck W. and Thelen K. (2005) *Beyond Continuity: Institutional Change in Advanced Political Economies*, Oxford, Oxford University Press.

Wright V. (1996) 'The National Coordination of European Policy-Making: Negotiating the Quagmire', in Richardson J. (ed.), *European Union: Power and Policy-Making*, London, Routledge (148–169).

Xiros T. (2006) 'The Participation of Greece in the EU 1981–2005. Government and Governmental Bodies', *International and European Policy* (3) (159–178) [in Greek].

3 EU coordination in Ireland

Centralization to master the crisis

Brigid Laffan

1 Introduction

When Ireland joined the then European Communities (ECs) in 1973, an additional layer of governance was added to its domestic system of policy-making, requiring adaptation of its national political and administrative systems. The national core executive, that is, the Irish Government and central administration or bureaucracy became a dominant carrier of Europeanization, as the system was required to adjust to engagement with the European Union's (EU's) system of collective governance (Featherstone and Radaelli 2003, 334). Adaptation to EU membership required more than just a one-off adjustment as the EU polity expanded and evolved over time both in terms of the scope of its activities and its constitutional architecture. The Irish core executive became the bridge between the national and the European in the EU's networked system of governance, with members of the Government and senior civil service officials, the *cadre* or boundary managers, acting as translators of EU policies, norms, and practices into the domestic arena and projecting domestic preferences back into the EU arena (Bulmer and Burch 1998, 2000, and 2001; Genschel 2001; Featherstone and Radaelli 2003). Managing Brussels became increasingly central to the Irish core executive. This was greatly accentuated in the period following the 2008 financial crisis and particularly during Ireland's period as a programme country from 2010 to 2013. This chapter provides an overview of how Ireland's approach evolved and then focuses on the post-crisis period.

2 Origins and development of the management of EU issues in Ireland[1]

From accession to the EU in 1973 to the end of the 1990s, Ireland's system for managing EU business was relatively stable. The structures and processes put in place when Ireland joined to position Ireland in the EU system appeared to work well over time, and change, when it occurred, was incremental and adaptive to developments at the EU level. Successive rounds of treaty change brought new domestic actors into the management system and increased the amount of EU business that had to be addressed. At the same time, a subtle shift occurred with the enhancement of the Prime Minister's (PM; *Taoiseach* in Irish) position as overall guide and steerer of Irish EU policy. In 2001, however, a domestic critical juncture occurred with the 'No' vote to the Nice Treaty by the Irish electorate. The negative vote triggered a period of review and evaluation and resulted in significant change in how EU business was and is managed in Ireland (Laffan and O'Mahony 2007 and 2008).

The period between the country's accession in January 1973 and the end of its first Presidency in December 1975 was Ireland's apprenticeship in the European system. During this period, the Irish Government put in place structures and processes for managing the relationship with Brussels. In its fundamentals, the management system put in place remained unchanged until the late 1980s. Responsibility for day-to-day coordination on EU matters was assigned to the Ministry of Foreign Affairs (MFA) and the principle of the 'lead ministry' was firmly established. In this way, the lead ministry became the domestic interlocutor with the EU and was responsible from the outset for coordinating preparations for Council meetings falling within their remit (Kassim 2003, 98). Overall, there was very little institution-building in the form of new structures; rather, there was a reliance on the adaptation of existing domestic structures within the broad parameters of collective responsibility and ministerial responsibility. The Irish administration faced the challenge of adapting to the Brussels system with limited human resources. The preparations for the first Presidency in 1975 were important for Ireland's adjustment to EU membership as the demands of running a Presidency ensured that ministerial responsibility for different policy areas was clearly delineated and management of Council business meant that ministers and officials became familiar with the nuts and bolts of the Union's policy process across all policy areas. Indeed, the experience of the Presidency had an important effect on the psychological environment of national policy-makers: thereafter, the Union became an accepted albeit complicating factor in national decision-making.

The resurgence of formal integration in the EU level from the late 1980s onwards led to change in the Irish system. With the signature of the Single European Act (SEA), the negotiation of the Delors I multi-annual budgetary package, and the ratification of the Maastricht Treaty, the amount of EU business to be dealt with increased dramatically as did its range. New domestic players became involved in the EU game. With increased policy-making in areas such as environment and internal security, the Ministries of Environment and Justice moved from being peripheral actors to key ministries involved in managing EU business and cross-cutting issues. The growing importance of the European Council in EU policy-making enhanced the position of the Irish PM in determining the broad contours of Ireland's EU policy. Under the premiership of Charles Haughey in particular (1987–1991), the Office of the PM adopted a stronger leadership and played a key role in negotiating and implementing Ireland's first national development plan using the increased structural funds gained from the Delors I package. The hitherto moribund interministerial European Communities Committee was rejuvenated by the Office of the PM and chaired by a new Minister of State for European Affairs. A high level committee of ministers and senior civil servants was also established and serviced by the Office of the PM. These committees were never fully formalized, however, and subsequently relied on prime ministerial will for their existence. Finally, the dominance of the executive in the management of EU business weakened the already limited role of Parliament in monitoring Irish EU policy and added to the process of deparliamentarization evident in political systems throughout Europe (Kassim 2003, 91).

The electorate's decision to reject the Nice Treaty in 2001 shook the Irish executive system for the management of EU business to its core. Until 2001, Ireland had managed to portray itself as a constructive player in the Union with a relatively *communautaire* approach in general. The desire to be seen as broadly *communautaire* led successive Irish governments to go with the emerging EU consensus unless an issue was highly sensitive.[2] The 'No' to Nice and the low turnout in the referendum (34 per cent) of the electorate highlighted the fact that the hitherto benign domestic environment towards the EU would not continue and the Government could no longer take its voters for granted. Ireland's European policy was loose of its moorings, which in turn led to considerable soul searching at the official and political level of how EU business was managed and how Europe was portrayed at the national level.

With the rejection of the Nice Treaty, Ireland's core executive reached a critical juncture in its management of EU business and a number of key structural and procedural reforms were set in train as a response (most notably the 'ratcheting-up' of interministerial coordination and enhanced parliamentary scrutiny). These reforms helped contribute to the success of Ireland's sixth EU Presidency from January to June 2004 and the final negotiation of the EU's constitutional treaty under the Irish watch.

3 The core executive

The structures of the Irish core executive that deal with EU business include: the ministries, committees, and designated units with responsibility for managing EU affairs. Given the reach of EU policies on national policy-making, every ministry and office in the Irish core executive system is required to deal with the EU in some way. The extent of interaction and need to manage EU business depends primarily on the degree of Europeanization found in the respective policy domains of each office and ministry. The Irish core executive system's management of EU business involves three distinct gradations based on this criterion: the hub of EU management, the inner core, and the outer circle.

The salience of the EU in the particular policy area determines the response of the individual ministries in setting up structures to deal with the flow of EU business. Three overarching administrations – Ministry of Foreign Affairs (MFA), Ministry of Finance (MF), and the Office of the PM – managed Irish EU policy from a macro perspective and were considered the central structural nodes through which Ireland's overall EU strategy must pass at varying stages. These three administrations have been referred to as the 'Holy Trinity' of Ireland's management of EU business (Laffan 2001). At the second level, or the inner core, EU policies are central or increasingly central to the work undertaken by the Ministries of Agriculture, Justice, Enterprise, Trade and Employment, and the Environment. Given its responsibility for the implementation of all European law into domestic law, the Office of the Attorney General is also included in this level. As EU competence grew from the 1980s onwards in new policy areas such as environment and internal security, and more hands-on involvement in the formulation, coordination, and monitoring of new legislation was necessary, some ministries (namely Justice and Environment) moved from the outer circle to the inner core. For the ministries in the outer circle of core-executive management, coordinating and managing national policy remains the overarching concern. However, each of these ministries, to varying degrees, deals with a certain amount of EU business; particularly as they have become involved in the Lisbon agenda.

3.1 The 'Holy Trinity': Ministry of Foreign Affairs, Office of the PM, and Ministry of Finance

The MFA assumed the role of lead ministry on EU matters from the MF in 1973. Its place at the heart of the Irish core executive is still taken as given; however, it now shares its coordinating responsibilities to a greater degree with the Office of the PM. In September 1973, the MFA issued its main circular that established how EU business should be handled (CH/177/35). Responsibility for day-to-day coordination on EU matters was assigned to the MFA. This constituted a break with the past, as the MF had been the lead ministry in the period leading up to membership. Accession to the ECs in 1973 had a major impact on the structure of the MFA and was instrumental in promoting the modernization of the Irish Foreign Service (Keatinge 1995, 2). The Ministry's modernization was characterized by an increase in the number of staff in head office and in Irish missions abroad.

Increased resources were accompanied by internal organizational changes with the creation of new divisions, the reorganization of existing ones and increased functional specialization at the head office. Those changes were a response to membership, the demands of managing a presidency, and the widening scope and reach of Irish foreign policy. In the late 1980s, the MFA, like all ministries, suffered a reduction in staff during the public sector recruitment embargo. However, concern about the capacity of headquarters to direct the growing diplomatic network and to respond to the demands of strategic policy-making led to a major internal review of its resources and organizational structure in 1999–2000. The *chef de file* or lead unit arrangement, where each unit within the Ministry has overall responsibility for particular regions or countries of the world, was put in place in February 2002.

Within the Irish system, the MFA is the Ministry with an overview of developments in the EU from an institutional and political perspective. In addition, its embassies in the Member States can provide information and briefing on the policy positions of these States. The Irish Permanent Representation in Brussels is a pivotal source of intelligence on developments in the EU and has a key function in identifying how and what national preferences can be promoted within the EU and in identifying the trade-offs that might be necessary as negotiations develop. The Permanent Representative in Brussels is always one of Ireland's most senior and experienced diplomats. The Permanent Representation's role is to engage with its counterparts in the Committee of Permanent Representatives (COREPER) II and to support ministers in the Council of Ministers and the PM in the European Council. The Permanent Representative plays a very important role in advising Dublin on Brussels-level developments and in creating negotiating strategies in conjunction with colleagues at home (McDonagh 2015).

The MFA's Europe Division coordinates Ireland's approach within the EU in close cooperation with the EU Division of the Office of the PM, while the Political Division of the MFA is responsible for international political issues and manages Ireland's participation in the EU's Common Foreign Security Policy and defence issues. The Europe Division and the Irish Representation in Brussels form two central nodes in the management of EU business as they interact with a) EU institutions, particularly the Council, but also the Commission and Parliament, and b) Government ministries (both individually and collectively).

The Department of the PM, while small in size compared to other ministries, is central to the conduct of EU business, as it serves as the secretariat to the PM. Its role in the conduct of EU business has been considerably enhanced in recent years to the extent that it is now considered as one of the two 'EU coordinating departments' (Interview Official 62, 26.03.2002). While primary responsibility for the development of Ireland's European policy on specific issues rests with individual ministries, the core role of the Department of the PM is to provide a strategic direction and focus for this European policy in overall terms. The aim of those in the Department is to work in tandem with the relevant line ministries rather than duplicate the work already being done. The relatively small size of the Department of the PM necessitates this approach. The Department can be brought into any set of negotiations if they become problematic or in the event of deep-rooted interministerial conflict. The tendency is 'to delegate and to coordinate as required and not to micro-manage' (Interview Official 49, 12.02.2002).

The MF's role in EU business increased significantly from the mid-1980s with the Single Market programme, EU structural and cohesion funds, taxation, and the Economic and Monetary Union (EMU); it could now be said to have an interest in everything European for its role as the controller of the public finances gives it a central role in EU affairs. It is standard practice that EU proposals with financial implications for the Exchequer must be cleared with the MF before being approved. The Ministry plays a major role in negotiations on taxation, where the MFA's involvement is minimal. The two Divisions of the MF centrally involved in EU business are the Banking, Finance and International Services Division (BFID) and the Budget and Economic Division (BED). These sections have autonomy and responsibility for policy in respect of issues under their aegis and pull together when attending the Economic and Financial Affairs Council (ECOFIN).

In summary, the roles of the three bodies in the core of the system are complementary rather than competitive. The Department of the PM brings the authority of the PM to bear on cross-cutting issues, and meetings called by this Department will always be taken seriously. The MFA brings its knowledge of the EU, its negotiating expertise, and its knowledge of the attitudes of other Member States to the table. These two are major players in all of the macro-negotiations and have very close relations on the management of EU business. The MF is less involved in macro-issues regarding the development of the EU but is central to all aspects of economic governance.

4 Coordination of EU policies

The coordination ambition depends on the nature of the issue on the Brussels agenda, the phase of the policy process, and the national style in managing

EU business. A fourfold distinction between routine sectoral policy-making, major policy shaping decisions within sectors, cross-sectoral issues, and the big bargains is apposite. Ministries can handle the routine business of dealing with Brussels within clearly defined sectoral areas without engaging in too much interministerial consultation and coordination. In addition, the Irish system gives individual ministries considerable autonomy within their own sectors even on the major shaping issues provided the wider system is kept informed. On the key national priorities, the Irish system engages in 'selective centralization' (Kassim 2003). The system will channel political and administrative resources on the big issues. This has occurred on a number of occasions when big issues demanded an interministerial coordinated response, e.g. the 1983 negotiations on the reform of the Common Agricultural Policy,[3] the 1996 and 2004 EU Presidencies, and the 1999 multi-annual budgetary negotiations (Agenda 2000).

4.1 Horizontal coordination

In all Member States, committees at different levels in the hierarchy play a central role in the interministerial or horizontal coordination of EU affairs. They are the main institutional devices for formal horizontal coordination. Until 2001, a key characteristic of the Irish committee system was its institutional fluidity and malleability. The cabinet is the centre of political decision-making in the Irish system. It processes EU issues according to the same standard operating procedures and rules that govern the processing of domestic issues. Although under-institutionalized by Continental standards, the substructure of the Irish cabinet has been strengthened by the establishment of a series of cabinet subcommittees, including an EU Committee. The latter is attended by the key ministers with an EU brief, ministerial advisors, and senior civil servants. In preparation for the 2004 Presidency, this EU Committee met once every two weeks and was chaired by the PM.

Following the first Nice referendum defeat, the Irish committee system became embedded in the Irish system with formalization of the interministerial coordination (chaired by the Minister of State for European Affairs). Senior officials attend the EU Committee from each ministry, as can the Permanent Representative. The Committee is used as an early warning system for potentially problematic issues arising out of EU business, as well as a forum to facilitate strategic thinking across government ministries. As in the cabinet subcommittee, the practice of holding presentations on relevant issues also takes place within the EU Committee. Senior officials from government ministries attend a number of other, generally *ad hoc*, interministerial committees designed to deal with specific cross-cutting issues that arise.

4.2 The Permanent Representation

The Permanent Representation is an integral part of Ireland's management of EU business. It is a microcosm of Ireland's core executive in Brussels and its staff maintains very close links with their home ministries in Dublin. Traditionally, staff numbers had always been small (in the 1990s Ireland had the second smallest Permanent Representation in the EU). However, a significant increase in staffing occurred in the 1990s, when a number of domestic ministries felt the need for a presence in Brussels. By the 2004 Presidency, staff numbered more than 140 (including military staff). The incremental process of Europeanization is evident in the number of ministries that have a presence in the Representation. In 1973, six ministries had staff in Brussels. A further three ministries joined them in the late 1970s and 1980s. In the 1990s and onwards, the Ministries of the Marine (1991), Justice (1995), Health (1996), the Office of the Attorney General (1999), Defence (2000), Education (2001), Arts, Culture and the Gaeltacht (2002) were added to the list. All domestic ministries with the exception of the Department of the PM are now represented in Brussels. Officials at the Representation regard servicing the Council as their core business, and the cycle of the Council, COREPER, and working party business sets the tempo of work in the Representation (Laffan 2001, 289). According to one former Ambassador, 'the major job of the Permanent Representative is to ask "is this something we can win?" and "what will I advise the Minister?"' (Interview Official 55, 07.03.2002). During negotiations, especially those of a sensitive nature, there is continuous and high-level contact between the Dublin ministries, the MFA, and Brussels on the stance Ireland should take.

4.3 Executive-parliamentary relations

Until the critical juncture of the first Nice Treaty referendum defeat in June 2001, the relationship between Parliament (*Oireachtas*) and the core executive was weak. Relations between Parliament and the EU had been characterized as a combination of neglect and ignorance (O'Halpin 1996, 124). On accession, a Joint Parliament Committee on the Secondary Legislation of the ECs was established as a 'watchdog committee'. However, its performance was modest, hampered as it was by limited resources and lack of interest by parliamentary deputies and the media in its output. In 1993, it was reconstituted as the Joint Parliament Committee on European Affairs and its primary role was to inform deputies and senators of general EU policy developments rather than scrutinize EU legislation as such.

The weakness or perceived absence of parliamentary scrutiny of EU business was highlighted as a serious problem during the 2001 Nice referendum.

In response to this, the Government developed a new system of enhanced parliamentary scrutiny of EU affairs codified in the 2002 EU Scrutiny Act. The parliamentary link for the new procedures is the EU Scrutiny Subcommittee of the Joint Parliament Committee for European Affairs. All EU-related documents are deposited in the MFA's EU Coordination Unit and passed on to relevant ministries to prepare briefing notes. These briefing notes are then transmitted to the EU Scrutiny Subcommittee to be examined on a two-weekly basis. With the help of a policy advisor, the Subcommittee identifies EU legislative proposals that are significant enough to merit parliamentary scrutiny by the relevant sectoral or ministerial parliamentary committees. The relevant committee then produces a report on its deliberations, which is laid before Parliament. While the proposals make provision for extensive engagement between Parliament, ministers, and officials, a binding scrutiny reserve has not been put in place. Instead, ministers are honour-bound to take the opinion of the relevant committee into account when negotiating in the Council of Ministers. Differences of opinion have been extremely rare as a high degree of consensus exists between the sectoral committees and ministries (Interview Official 78, 27.10.2005, and Joint Committee on European Affairs Subcommittee on European Scrutiny, Second Annual Report 2005). Following the original circular on the management of EU business in 1973, the guidelines on parliamentary scrutiny are the next most significant formalization of the management of EU business in Ireland. The need for the ministries to prepare notes for the corresponding Parliament Committees has ensured that within each ministry, formal systems must be put in place to ensure that such notes are prepared.

5 The crisis hit

The Irish crisis began in September 2008 when the Government agreed to guarantee the liabilities of the Irish banks without knowing what the full extent of those liabilities were. This followed the June rejection of the Lisbon Treaty by the Irish electorate. Ireland's European policy was again under stress, as the Government had to cope with the twin challenges of the Lisbon defeat and the banking crisis. When the global financial crisis morphed into a Eurozone crisis in autumn 2009 and the situation in Greece deteriorated, Ireland became very vulnerable as concern about the state of the Irish financial system was felt in rising spreads. Finally, in November 2010, under extreme pressure from the European Central Bank (ECB) and other Member States, Ireland became the second Euro State to receive a bail-out. Spreads on Irish bonds had reached 9 per cent, which was unsustainable and resulted in Ireland losing its market access. This meant that Ireland became a programme country subject to a

Memorandum of Understanding (MoU) with the Troika (International Monetary Fund (IMF), European Central Bank (ECB), European Commission) – which made Ireland a dependent rather than an interdependent State. This was a major shock to the Irish State elite, as the country had always been able to access the financial markets. The response to the economic downturn was already well in train before the arrival of the Troika. The MoU was largely based on an internally generated plan which was added to but not determined by the Troika.

The financial package negotiated with the Troika amounted to 85 billion Euros, of which 17.5 billion came from domestic sources. The programme had three elements: financial-sector reform, fiscal consolidation, and structural reform. The first two programme elements were the most significant, as the Irish economy was both open and flexible, and was not faced with the level of structural reforms found in other programme States. The incumbent Government inevitably paid the electoral price in the elections on 25 February 2011: the Fianna Fail-led Government was roundly defeated in the polls and replaced by a Fine Gael-Labour coalition that took office on 9 March 2011. The Fianna Fail-Green Party coalition that had governed through the crisis up to the election had effectively been fire-fighting, reeling under the uncertainty of the situation in the banks, and facing a deteriorating fiscal and economic situation. In the end, the coalition appeared unable to manage the magnitude of the multiple crises it faced – economic, fiscal, financial, political, and reputational.

Ireland's approach to being a programme country consisted of a number of different strands, only one of which was administrative reform. First, a strong emphasis was placed on repairing Ireland's international reputation. The State system went into overdrive in reaching out to important international stakeholders and influencers. Secondly, the Irish diaspora was seen as a major resource in repairing the damage done by the bubble and bust cycle. Thirdly, another emphasis was placed on ensuring that highly competent individuals assumed roles in the Central Bank and the Financial Regulator's office; new appointments were also made in the MF. Thus, changing human agency, not just institutions, was central to understanding the Irish response. Fourthly, a commitment was made to democratic renewal in the Programme for Government. Fifthly, the new Government divided the MF into two in February 2011, with one arm focused on the traditional role of a finance ministry and the other on reform. The two ministries were called the Ministry of Public Expenditure and Reform, and the Ministry of Finance (MF). In addition, the Government set up an Economic Management Council (EMC) and altered the coordination of EU affairs.

The new Government that took office in March 2011 did so with the largest electoral mandate of any Government in Irish history. The basis for government was the agreed 'Programme for Government', a programme for national recovery, and the MoU that Ireland had signed with the Troika. The Government Programme was replete with references to constitutional and political reforms. There was also a major emphasis on restoring Ireland's international reputation. With respect to the core executive, the programme claimed that: 'A key condition of a successful turn-around strategy for the country is a more joined-up strategic centre at the heart of government, with the power to confront and break up the concentrations of power that so damaged the country' (see Fine Gael 2011).

The strategic centre at the heart of Government emerged as the Economic Management Council (EMC), consisting of the four most senior ministers in Government: the Prime Minister, Deputy Prime Minister, and the Ministers for Finance and Public Expenditure. These four senior office holders, together with their advisors and a select number of senior officials, formed the strategic core of the response to the crisis. A second Secretary General was appointed to the Office of the PM to oversee the work of the EMC. The Minister of Public Expenditure suggested that it was 'the decision-making nexus for all economic policy'. Replying to a parliamentary question on 13 April 2011, the PM said that:

> The Economic Management Council will deal with economic planning and budgetary matters, with the economic recovery programme, including the representation of Ireland internationally in negotiations with the EU, the ECB, the IMF, and the Troika, the integration of the work of Departments and agencies, and the coordination of banking policy.

By then, just one month into its existence, the EMC, which held the status of a cabinet subcommittee, had met 10 times. It was the key strategic nexus for managing the public finances during a period of harsh fiscal consolidation. It also acted as the centre for the management of the coalition Government, as it involved the most senior ministers from both parties. Yet the EMC was not a traditional cabinet subcommittee but more akin to a war council, representing the collective leadership within the Government.

Following the 2016 elections, the PM announced that the EMC would not be continued under the new Government. This reflected the return of growth to the Irish economy and the restoration of the Irish public finances. It confirms the fact that the EMC had been a war cabinet, a once-off centralization that reflected the severity of the crisis faced by Ireland. The shift of responsibility for the EU business to the Office of the PM proved more enduring. Because of the intersection of EU, Troika, and domestic policy, the then second Secretary responsible for the EMC was also the lead coordinator of EU affairs and accompanied the PM to all European Councils and meetings with other heads of State. This represented a shift in EU responsibility. Traditionally, EU coordination had been shared between the Office of the PM and the MFA, but it was finally moved to the Office of the PM. The MFA retained responsibility for the external dimension of EU policy, enlargement, and relations with Member States, but the Office of the PM became the nerve centre of the high politics of the Troika and the European Council.

The new Ministry of Public Expenditure and Reform, the MF, and the Office of the PM became the new 'Holy Trinity' in charge of managing the Irish programme and Ireland's engagement with the Troika and the EU through the EMC. Their role was to manage the country through the severe multidimensional crisis it faced and deal with both the domestic and international dimensions of this. In addition to fiscal consolidation and the banking crisis, the new Government was determined to renegotiate the terms with the Troika and the reduction in the minimum wage. Both these goals were achieved by July 2011, when Ireland negotiated a lowering of the rate and was permitted to reverse the minimum-wage reduction.

The budgetary process was a major focus of reform as Ireland together with all Member States had to implement the new rules on economic governance and ratify the Stability Pact (Treaty on Stability, Coordination and Growth, TSCG). The Stability Pact was put to a referendum in May 2012 and accepted by the people. The Fiscal Responsibility Act 2012 provided a statutory basis for the Fiscal Council (the Council had been operating without a statutory basis from June 2011) to advise the Government on budgetary policy and made provision for the new budgetary rules. It consists of five members of international standing who sit on the Council for four years. Its independence is protected both by law and an independent budget. The impact of the changes in economic governance is to alter the calendar and cycle of budgetary policy by beginning much earlier every year (publication of the Stability Programme Update in April) instead of beginning in the autumn, by engaging with Parliament at an earlier stage, and moving the big set piece, budget speech from December to mid-October 2015. In the Irish case, the new system of economic governance serves to lengthen, formalize, and render more transparent the budgetary process. This should in time foster better budgetary planning and more parliamentary oversight in addition to the greater intrusion of the Commission in the domestic budgetary cycle.

A major preoccupation of the Irish Government was the cost to the Irish taxpayer of the bank bail-out (circa 64 billion Euros) and the fact that bondholders were repaid in full. The IMF favoured a bail-in of unsecured bondholders in the Irish case but was overruled by the two European institutions, the ECB and the Commission, with ECB President Trichet taking a particularly strong stand. Some of the refinancing of the Irish banks involved what became known as promissory notes. Ireland sought a reduction in the costs of servicing the notes. It engineered an *ad hoc* solution in 2012 but pressed the matter during Ireland's seventh Council Presidency in 2013. This issue was so important for the Government that it was unwilling to delay pressure for change and a better deal until after the Presidency. When the Anglo-Irish Bank failed and was taken into public ownership together with another smaller financial institution, it became known as the Irish Bank Resolution Corporation (IBRC). IBRC was funded by credit from the Irish Central Bank based on an Irish State guarantee with the approval of the Board of the ECB. This funding meant that international bondholders and creditors in other States were paid and did not suffer losses. The funding mechanism envisaged repayments of approximately three billion Euros by the Irish State every year to 2022. This was highly controversial because the Irish public was furious at repaying international bondholders and the annual payment of three billion Euros was on top of a programme of severe fiscal consolidation and austerity. Finding a solution to the promissory note problem was a major strategic aim of the Irish Government and Central Bank. In the first half of the Presidency, the Irish Finance Minister, Michael Noonan, continued to press for an agreement to alter the nature of the promissory notes. In the teeth of considerable opposition, including from Germany, the Government succeeded in achieving an outcome in March. The promissory notes were replaced by long-term bonds ranging from twenty-seven to forty years maturity, which had a positive impact on the flow of Irish debt. Notwithstanding this success, legacy bank debt remains a concern in Ireland and the Government continues to negotiate with the Troika for less strict conditions with little traction. Although Irish society acknowledges that Ireland must pay a price for weak financial regulation, there is deep anger about the lack of burden-sharing, as financial regulation was similarly weak in the lending/creditor countries.

6 Conclusion

The financial crisis that began in September 2008 and the defeat of the Lisbon referendum in June 2008 combined to undermine Ireland's position as a stable constructive Member State of the EU. The referendum was reversed in October 2009, when the Irish electorate was confronted with the depth of the domestic crisis. It took much longer for the acute phase of the financial crisis to subside. Between September 2008 and November 2010, the Irish Government struggled to address the fragility of its banking system, the deterioration of its fiscal position, and a worsening economy. It failed to contain the crisis and had to succumb to a programme. This led to the collapse of the Government and its replacement by a centre-left coalition in 2011. The new Government moved quickly to greatly strengthen the core executive and the inner cabinet, in the form of the Economic Management Council (EMC), which was the core that established the strategy and tactics to move Ireland beyond the bail-out. It consisted of four senior ministers, including the PM, and a core of senior civil servants. This group acted like a taskforce to oversee the international and domestic dimensions of Ireland's crisis strategy. The division of the Ministry of Finance into a Ministry of Finance and a Ministry of Public Expenditure and Reform was the second major change in the Irish core executive. The fact that the EMC was discontinued following the 2016 General Election underlines the adaptable and flexible nature of the Irish system of public administration and governance. During the course of the crisis, the Office of the PM took over as the lead coordinator for EU business, which reduced the role of the MFA in the core executive. This accelerated trends that were apparent in the system before the crisis, especially the growing role of the European Council in EU affairs. In addition to institutional changes, all of the most senior civil servants were replaced, and a new Governor of the Irish Central Bank and a new Financial Regulator were appointed. Beyond the core executive, a Fiscal Council was established in June 2011 and given a statutory basis in 2012. The priorities with regard to EU policy and politics were to fulfil the terms of the MoU, consolidate Ireland's fiscal position, prepare for and run Ireland's seventh Presidency in 2013, and successfully exit the bail-out in December 2013 without a credit line.

The Irish State elite responded to the crisis within the operating procedures of the political and administrative culture. The reflex was to bring in new people, strengthen the core executive, reform the civil and public service, repair Ireland's reputation, and negotiate with Ireland's partners. There is a determination to continue to negotiate better terms on the loans and to Europeanize the legacy of the bank debt, if possible. Lately, it has not been possible to distinguish between the domestic and the EU. The strengths of the Irish State were in evidence: adaptability, flexibility, and a focus on a limited number of core issues. However, serious political reform promised by this Government has not materialized and many questions remain about the depth of public-service reform.

Notes

1 This section draws on Laffan and O'Mahony 2007, 2008.
2 It has been said that Irish Governments agreed to projects such as economic and monetary union and foreign and security policy reforms in return for increased structural funds, a strategy termed 'conditionally integrationist' (Scott 1994).

3 The so-called 'super-levy' negotiations where quotas were placed limiting the amount of food, milk, etc. that farmers could produce in return for financial receipts.

Bibliography

Agenda 2000 of the Commission of the EU.

Bulmer S. and Burch M. (1998) 'Organizing for Europe: Whitehall, the British State and the European Union', *Public Administration* 76 (4) (601–628).

Bulmer S. and Burch M. (2000) 'The Europeanization of British Central Government', in Rhodes R.A.W. (ed.), *Transforming British Government Volume 1*, London, Macmillan.

Bulmer S. and Burch M. (2001) 'The Europeanization of Central Government: The UK and Germany in Historical Institutionalist Perspective', in Aspinwall M.D. and Schneider G. (eds.), *The Rules of Integration*, Manchester, Manchester University Press.

Department of Taoiseach (2011) *Programme for Government 2011–2016*, http://www.taoiseach.gov.ie/eng/Work_Of_The_Department/Programme_for_Government/Programme_for_Government_2011-2016.pdf .

Featherstone K. and Radaelli C. (eds.) (2003) *The Politics of Europeanization*, Oxford, Oxford University Press.

Fine Gael (2011) *Reinventing Government: Protecting Services and Getting the Economy Back on Track*, Dublin, Fine Gael.

Genschel P. (2001) 'Comment: The Europeanization of Central Government', in Aspinwall M.D. and Schneider G. (eds.), *The Rules of Integration*, Manchester, Manchester University Press.

Joint Committee on European Affairs Subcommittee on European Scrutiny (2005) *Second Annual Report on the Operation of the European Union (Scrutiny) Act 2002: 1 January 2004 to 31 December 2004*, Dublin, Government Publications.

Kassim H. (2003) 'Meeting the Demands of EU Membership: The Europeanization of National Administrative Systems', in Featherstone K. and Radaelli C. (eds.), *The Politics of Europeanization*, Oxford, Oxford University Press (83–111).

Keatinge P. (1995) 'The Irish Foreign Service: An Observer's View', *Seminar on the Irish Foreign Service*, 2 March, Trinity College.

Laffan B. (2001) *Organising for a Changing Europe: Irish Central Government and the European Union*, Trinity College Dublin, Policy Institute.

Laffan B. (2003) *Managing Europe from Home. Impact of the EU on Executive Government: A Comparative Analysis*, http://www.oeue.net/papers/acomparativeanalysis-theimpact.pdf.

Laffan B. and O'Mahony J. (2007) 'Managing Europe from an Irish Perspective: Critical Junctures and the Increasing Formalization of the Core Executive in Ireland', *Public Administration* 85 (1) (167–188).

Laffan B. and O'Mahony J. (2008) *Ireland and the European Union*, Basingstoke, Palgrave Macmillan.

McDonagh B. (2015) 'Inside the Mind of a Permanent Representative in Brussels: Personal Reflections', Florence, EUI Working Paper RSCAS 2015/50.

O'Halpin E. (1996) 'Irish Parliamentary Culture and the EU: Formalities to be Observed', in Norton P. (ed.), *National Parliaments and the European Union*, London, Frank Cass.

Scott D. (1994) *Ireland's Contribution to the European Union*, Dublin, Institute for European Affairs.

Thelen K. (1999) 'Historical Institutionalism in Comparative Politics', *Annual Review of Political Science* 2 (369–404).

Wessels W., Mauer A. and Mittag J. (eds.) (2003) *Fifteen into One? The European Union and Its Member States*, Manchester, Manchester University Press.

4 EU coordination in Portugal

Continuity and flexibility in a Troika regime

José Magone

1 Introduction

On 17 May 2014, Portugal successfully completed the strict Economic Adjustment Programme agreed upon with the Troika (European Central Bank [ECB], the International Monetary Fund [IMF], and European Commission) three years earlier. This interference in Portuguese national sovereignty was regarded as a major debacle for the Portuguese political class. Both the incumbent Socialist Party (*Partido Socialista, PS*) as well as the main opposition parties, the Social Democrats (*Partido Social Democrata*, PSD) and the Democratic Social Centre-People's Party (*Centro Democrático Social-Partido Popular*, CDS-PP), had to sign the agreement and comply with the austerity measures included in the document. Portugal left the Troika regime after Ireland in 2013. By now, Cyprus has also left the Troika regime, and Greece alone remains under its close supervision.

The sovereign debt crisis and the Euro crisis have for the first time challenged the perception by the Portuguese political class and population that the European Union (EU) is a purely benevolent actor (Magone 2014b, 347–348). In fact, the crises showed that sound financial and fiscal policies are of the utmost importance for the survival of a small country in a globalized economy. Portugal was able to join the first wave of members to the Economic and Monetary Union (EMU) in 1999 (Torres 1998; Torres 2000). This was due to a strict adherence to the so-called Maastricht criteria, the most important of these were a budget deficit below 3 per cent of gross domestic product (GDP) and a public debt below 60 per cent of GDP. However, already in 2001, Portugal began to struggle with keeping the deficit below 3 per cent; therefore, it became the first country to endure the Excessive Deficit Procedure (EDP) for excessive deficit. Between 2001 and 2011, the country's deficit hovered above or around 3 per cent of GDP due to a stagnating economy with no growth, and sometimes negative growth. Any growth after 1993 was achieved by public investment in 'non-transactionable' goods alone (Torres 2009; Magone 2014b).

In spite of all these economic problems, the Portuguese national EU policy coordination system has been efficient and simple. Portuguese diplomacy in Brussels is able to preserve the country's main interest. In this sense, the main objective of this contribution is to investigate the national EU policy coordination structures before and after the sovereign debt crisis and to identify changes or transformations in the machinery. In the first section of this chapter, the strategic profile of Portuguese EU policy coordination is discussed. This is followed by a section on the making and, subsequently, on the workings of the machinery of policy coordination. A further section then discusses the changes that occurred after 2008. This is followed by a section on the mechanisms of domestic coordination adopted for the Economic and Financial Adjustment Programme (EFAP) agreed upon with the Troika. Finally, the chapter concludes with some observations on the continuity and flexibility of Portuguese EU policy coordination.

2 The strategic profile of Portuguese coordination of EU policy

Portugal may be regarded as matching one of the classification types of Hussein Kassim's typology of the national coordination of EU policy. Kassim differentiates between four types, following two dimensions of centralization and comprehensiveness. Portugal perfectly conforms with the 'centralized selective type' (Kassim 2015, 695; his categorization is based on Magone 2000). Parliament, interest groups, and civil society are rather side-lined in the Portuguese case; the country still has a very paternalistic form of decision-making, following very much the Napoleonic tradition of public administration.

The simplicity of the EU policy coordination machinery in Portugal emerged from trial and error, and through learning from the experiences of other Member States. It worked quite well for the purposes that Portugal set out to pursue. Portuguese diplomacy in European affairs is interested in protecting and fostering the national interest but at the same time also seeks to contribute to the integration process. Most of the time, the policy-coordinating structures merely coordinate the domestic positions in relation to policy areas that are not crucial for the country. In this sense, there is a high level of passivity in shaping the agenda: Portugal is rather an agenda and rule-taker than an agenda and rule-taker.

Portugal tends to passively download Europeanization packages. This was also true for the reform package related to the Troika regime, which was basically a concrete case of 'coercive Europeanization' (see Magone 2016). Uploading is a collective task, performed through alliances that endeavour to change negative conditions for the country; one example is the 2016 attempt by the Socialist minority Government under Prime Minister (PM) Antonio Costa to make changes to the Growth and Stability Pact by changing the rules of the game in alliance with France, Greece, and Italy (Börzel 2005). At least three reasons account for Portugal's role as an agenda and rule-taker.

First, Portugal is a small peripheral country with a low level of leverage in the EU. Second, Portugal does not have the human and material resources to develop original positions for all policy areas. However, the third and most important reason is that Portugal has decided to concentrate its input on issues of national strategic importance.

Among these issues are the regular negotiations of the Multiannual Financial Framework (MAFF). Portugal was part of the 'Club Med' in the 1980s and 1990s, and, after the EU's enlargement, became a proactive member of the 'Friends of Cohesion', which includes all Member States in Southern, Central, and Eastern Europe as well as Belgium. It is important for Portugal to keep the level of funding from the structural/cohesion funds at the same level as after the second doubling of the EU budget in 1992; this roughly equals 20 billion Euros. So far, Portugal has been largely successful in this matter. Although the country is strongly involved with the 'Friends of Cohesion' group, it has developed a flexible approach in creating alliances. Such alliances are established in the context of a 'structure of opportunities' approach, which means that different governments may search different alliances at different times. Due to the regular Iberian meetings at the heads-of-State level, a very close alliance exists with Spain in particular. Apart from cross-border cooperation and the cooperation in the management of common rivers, the alliance has also influence in the Eurozone, creating a common front of Southern European countries together with Italy and France.

A second issue consists in defending national interests in the intergovernmental conferences leading up to the European treaties. In this so-called 'treatyism', the Portuguese Government has been proactively engaged in grouping together the small States (population sizes of about 10 to 18 million) like Belgium, Hungary, the Czech Republic, the Netherlands, and Sweden to resist the shift of power to the larger States. This became particularly evident in the negotiations leading up to the Nice Treaty in December 2000.

A third issue is to use the Presidency of the EU to project a positive image of the country and put some issues of national strategic interest on the agenda. So far, the three presidencies of the EU were used to the fullest extent in order to be a proactive shaper of the European integration process (for further information see Cunha and Magone 2015).

Internally, EU policy has been so important for Portugal that it was de-politicized very quickly. Therefore, the administrative machinery dealing with EU national policy consists of extremely well-trained civil servants with strong linguistic skills and a professional approach to their work. Junior ministers have to work with these professionals, who normally push for a continuity of European policy-making.

In sum, following the typology of Hussein Kassim, Portuguese coordination of EU policy is quite centralized and selective in terms of policy-making, and is thereby similar to the models adopted by numerous small countries like Estonia, Ireland, Malta, Slovenia, but also Spain (Kassim 2015, 695).

3 The national EU policy coordination system

3.1 The making of the EU policy coordinating structures in Portugal

Portugal submitted its membership application on 28 February 1977. After a favourable opinion from the European Commission and the Council of Ministers of the European Communities in 1978, negotiations started formally on 17 September 1978; completion, however, took until 1980.

From the very beginning, a liaison structure to the European Communities' (ECs') institutions was established and was clearly destined to remain a prototype for the post-accession machinery. The national structure comprised the Commission of European Integration (*Comissão de Integração Europeia,* CIE), which was established on 3 August 1977 (decree-law 306), three months after the submission of the application (Correia 2006, 38), and based in Lisbon. The Commission had the status of a junior ministry (*secretáriado de estado*), and was assisted by a Secretariat of European Integration. Moreover, the embryonic structure of an interministerial coordinating committee, the so-called Group of Permanent Representatives (*grupo de representantes permanentes*), was set up to internally coordinate the positions of the ministries, the autonomous regions of Azores and Madeira, and the Bank of Portugal (*Banco de Portugal*) (Correia 2006, 40). In 1979, the Commission was further upgraded and renamed Secretariat of European Integration (*Secretariado de Integração Europeia,* SIE) following collaboration with the European Commission. The Secretariat, which assembled a strong team with a high level of expertise, became rather important for national coordination of EU policy. Due to the importance of European integration, successive governments gave considerable autonomy to the Secretariat, which was attached to the Office of the PM. According to one of the Secretariat's members, one of the main reasons was that the range of technical, political, and economic issues required a high level of coordination that only the core executive could ensure (Correia 2006, 38). However, the Office of the PM already delegated ECs-related issues to the

Ministry of Finance (MF) during the second Government of Mário Soares in the first half of 1978 (Correia 2006, 39).

Simultaneously, liaison structures were established in Brussels: the so-called Portuguese Delegation to the European Communities (*Delegação Portuguesa para as Comunidades Europeias*) was integrated into the structures of the Ministry of Foreign Affairs (MFA) before being renamed 'Mission' (*Missão Portuguesa junto das Comunidades Europeias*). According to the Chief of the Portuguese Mission in Brussels, Ernani Lopes, about twelve people worked in this structure in 1979 (Correia 2006, 40). In 1978, during the fourth Government – the second technocratic one appointed by President António Ramalho Eanes – a major restructuring took place. A new Vice Prime Minister of Economic Affairs and European Integration consolidated the coordinating structures related to European integration. He became the head of negotiations with the ECs, replacing the PM. A Council of Ministers on European integration was also introduced into the new structure through decree-law 185/79. Moreover, new coordinating units were established in the ministries that were more central to the European integration process (Correia 2006, 41). Government instability caused five changes in government between 1979 and 1985. The five governments (following the fourth Government) kept the Commission of European Integration intact; however, the Commission was allocated to different ministries on an almost yearly basis. In the fifth Government (1979), it was part of the Ministry of Economic Policy Coordination and Planning; in the sixth, it was part of the portfolio of the Vice Prime Minister, who was also Minister of Foreign Affairs. In the seventh Government, European integration was upgraded to an autonomous ministry; it lost this status in the subsequent eighth and ninth Governments, however.

In contrast, the Brussels delegation (or mission) always remained part of the MFA and the Commission of European Integration always remained the point of liaison.

In sum, in spite of governmental and economic instability, the coordination structures for negotiating European integration remained quite stable.

3.2 The establishment of a simple system

It took almost a decade for Portugal to become a member of the then European Communities (ECs) on 1 January 1986. In this period, the Portuguese political administration was able to gain a considerable amount of experience in dealing with European integration issues. Shortly before accession, the coordinating structures were transferred from the MF to the MFA by decree-law 526/85 of 31 December 1985. The main reason was the experience of the current Member States in their conduct of EC affairs; these States conferred the responsibility to coordinate internally and present externally the positions of the different sectoral interests of the State to the respective Ministry of Foreign Affairs. A junior ministry, the State Secretary of Community Affairs (*Secretariado do Estado de Integração Europeia,* SEIE), was also established. The new coordinating structure was called Directorate General of the European Communities (*Direcção Geral das Comunidades Europeias*, DGCE), replacing both the Commission of European Integration and the Secretariat of European Integration. Simultaneously, decree-law 459/85 of 4 November 1985 transformed the Portuguese Mission to the European Communities into the Permanent Representation to the ECs (*Representação Permanente junto ás Comunidades Europeias*, REPER). Central to the overall coordinating mechanism was the so-called Interministerial Committee of the European Communities (*Comissão Inter-ministerial das Comunidades Europeias*, CICE). Pursuant to decree-law 527/85 of 30 December 1985, the CICE was chaired by the Minister of Foreign Affairs or her representative, normally the Secretary of State of European Communities; it consisted of the ministers or their representatives and the representatives of the autonomous regions of Madeira and Azores. Other actors could also be invited to participate. The director of the Directorate General of European Communities was the Vice President. This structure remains much the same today. In spite of two major restructurings of the MFA in 1994 and 2006, the original model was maintained.

The presidencies of 1992, 2000, and 2007 in particular, all presented good opportunities to improve the quality of the coordinating structures. In 1990, the Council of Ministers for Community Affairs was revitalized in order to prepare for the Presidency. It was renamed the Council of Ministers of European Affairs (*Conselho de Ministros de Assuntos Europeus*) in 1998, shortly before the Presidency of the EU in 2000. In 1992, the Secretary of State of European Integration changed its name to Secretary of State of European Affairs (*Secretário do Estado de Assuntos Europeus*, SEAE). In 1994, the DGCE became the Directorate General for Community Affairs (*Direcção Geral para Assuntos Comunitários*, DGAC) (decree-law 48/94, Article 28) before finally becoming the Directorate General of European Affairs in 2006 (*Direcção Geral de Assuntos Europeus*, DGAE) (decree-law 204/2006, Article 12 and Article 27). Shortly before the crisis, Portugal was preparing for the Presidency of the EU in the second half of 2007. Moreover, the Socialist absolute-majority Government, which was in power between 2005 and 2011, introduced a major programme of restructuring that streamlined and slimmed down the DGAE. Some services dealing with EU Member States or candidate countries in the MFA were then integrated in the DGAE.

4 The working of the Portuguese coordination system of EU policy

4.1 The Directorate General of European Affairs: a highly sophisticated machine

As outlined above, the national coordination system of EU policy has not changed very much since its establishment in 1986. It is an extremely well-equipped mechanism that clearly has increased its efficiency over time. At the core of the policy coordination system is the DGAE, which supports the Secretary of State of European Affairs; both are part of the MFA. The DGAE consists of eight departments, each of which supervises several divisions. They are structured in order to ensure the Portuguese participation in the institutions of the EU. The main pluriannual objectives of the DGAE are fourfold:

> 1. ensuring the Portuguese participation in the institutions of the EU according to objectives established by the Government;
> 2. ensuring efficacy in the coordination of positions to be defended before the EU;
> 3. contributing to the participation in European construction by fostering national citizens' interest in European affairs through the provision of information;
> 4. ensuring the operational efficiency and efficacy of allocated resources.
>
> (DGAE 2013, 17)

All eight departments are geared towards very specific addressees internally and externally. These are the Assembly of the Republic, the PM, the Minister of Foreign Affairs, the Secretary of State for European Affairs, and all other secretaries of State of the MFA, the Permanent Representation, the internal and external services of the MFA, and the Portuguese Members of the European Parliament. Moreover, the organizations of civil society and the citizens in general are also addressees, particularly in relation to information on the EU and the participation of Portugal in the process of European construction, the management of European litigation due to the wrong application of the community rules and information on forthcoming competitions related to positions and internship in the EU institutions, including the allocation of scholarships to the Collège d'Europe and the European University Institute (EUI).

The structural tasks of the eight departments are shown in Table 4.1.

Outside the core coordinating structures, yet supporting them, is the European Information Centre Jacques Delors, originally co-funded by

Table 4.1 The core structure of the National EU Policy Coordination System in Portugal in the General-Directorate for European Affairs in Lisbon (2012)

<table>
<tr><td colspan="8">Director General</td></tr>
<tr><td colspan="3">Interministerial Committee of European Affairs (CIAE)</td><td colspan="2">Luso Portuguese Commission for Cross-border Cooperation</td><td>Interministerial Commission for Luso-Spanish Limits and Hidrographic Basins</td><td colspan="2"></td></tr>
<tr><td colspan="6">Number of Staff</td><td colspan="2"></td></tr>
<tr><td colspan="6">25</td><td colspan="2"></td></tr>
<tr><td colspan="3">Sub-director General</td><td colspan="3">Sub-director General</td><td colspan="2"></td></tr>
<tr><td colspan="3">3 Departments</td><td colspan="3">3 Departments</td><td colspan="2">2 Departments</td></tr>
<tr><td>Common Trade Policy</td><td>External European Relations and Enlargement</td><td>Economic and Financial Matters</td><td>Internal and Sectorial Policies</td><td>Justice and Home Affairs</td><td>Judicial Issues</td><td>Bilateral Relations</td><td>Institutional Affairs</td></tr>
<tr><td colspan="8">Number of Staff</td></tr>
<tr><td>9</td><td>13</td><td>9</td><td>16</td><td>8</td><td>14</td><td>7</td><td>7</td></tr>
<tr><td colspan="8">European Information Centre Jacques Delors</td></tr>
<tr><td colspan="8">Number of Staff</td></tr>
<tr><td colspan="8">19</td></tr>
<tr><td colspan="8">Total Number of Staff</td></tr>
<tr><td colspan="8">127</td></tr>
</table>

Source: DGAE 2013: 57–92

the European Commission, then incorporated into the DGAE in 2011. The Jacques Delors Centre has moved several times in the past years and the library is now based in the main building of the University of Lisbon and is open to the public. However, the archive and national documentation centre related to the DGAE is in the same place, in the Palace of Cova da Moura, which is close to the MFA.

Moreover, the national coordination system of EU policy did not escape the slimming-down and restructuring programme of public administration in Portugal through the Programme of Restructuring of State Central Administration (*Programa de Restruturação da Administração Central do Estado,* PRACE) between 2005 and 2011, a project co-funded by the EU (Diario de Noticias, 5 April 2011). Such restructuring was continued with the new Programme of Restructuring and Improvement of Central Administration (*Programa de restruturação e melhoria da administração central,* PREMAC) (Governo de Portugal 2012). If we compare the present structure to that of 2002, there has been a reduction from eleven to eight departments. Some areas such as agriculture and fisheries became part of the Department of Internal and Sectorial Policies. Moreover, the DGAE deals with all European matters as well as those related to countries outside the EU, such as the European Economic Area (EEA), the European Free Trade Area (EFTA), Switzerland, San Marino, and Andorra. Moreover, competences for economic policies related to the European space were transferred to the DGAE. The restructuring programmes have also led to the incorporation of two further commissions dealing with Portuguese-Spanish relations.

According to the 2011 report, PREMAC has led to a reduction of executive staff from twenty-nine to twenty-five, of top managing staff by one, and of intermediate level staff by three (DGAE 2013, 129). In total, the number of staff members in the DGAE was reduced to 127 from 165 between 2002 and 2012 (the latter by my own calculations, based on the MFA, Magone 2004, 67–75). However, the numbers have been quite stable since then. In 2010, there were 130 members of staff; one year later, the number was reduced to 122 before being increased again to 127 in 2012 (DGAE 2013, 127). The profile of the DGAE staff is characterized by employees who are highly qualified, specialized, and experienced in European issues. According to the DGAE, the average profile of a staff member is a woman in her fifties, with a higher education degree (*licenciatura*), a higher-ranking civil-service status, and a continuing contract (DGAE 2013, 127). In 2012, 72.4 per cent of staff members were women (DGAE 2013, 130). The technical and specialized character of the DGAE is proven by the expertise and professional profile that is inherent to 74 per cent of the employees. This is confirmed by the fact that 68 per cent of staff have a higher education degree, which is a stark comparison to the 15–17 per cent of the Portuguese population as a whole (DGAE, 2013: 126; see Figures 4.1 and 4.2).

The best civil servants and diplomats are allocated to this strategic department of the MFA.

The Secretary of State of European Affairs is a highly experienced diplomat or civil servant; it is a political position that changes with the alternation in government. During the Cavaco Silva (1985–1995) years, it was the highly experienced Vitor Martins; in the socialist Guterres Governments (1995–2001), it was the prestigious diplomat Francisco Seixas da Costa; in the Socrates Governments (2005–2011), it was Pedro Lourtie, who had previously been working in the Permanent Representation. In the Passos Coelho Government, the first Secretary of State between July 2011 and July 2013 was Miguel Morais Leitão, who had already acquired experience in the Barroso Government as Secretary of State of the Treasury. However, his successor, Bruno Maçães, came from the academic sector and is an outsider to the expert community of European affairs. He became known for his lack of sensitivity to diplomatic protocol and for going against protocol advice given by the Permanent Representative at the REPER. He clearly showed strong support for the position of Germany with regard to the austerity measures and aversion towards the South European alliance against austerity. This has led to a general alienation of the Portuguese position in relation to the other Southern

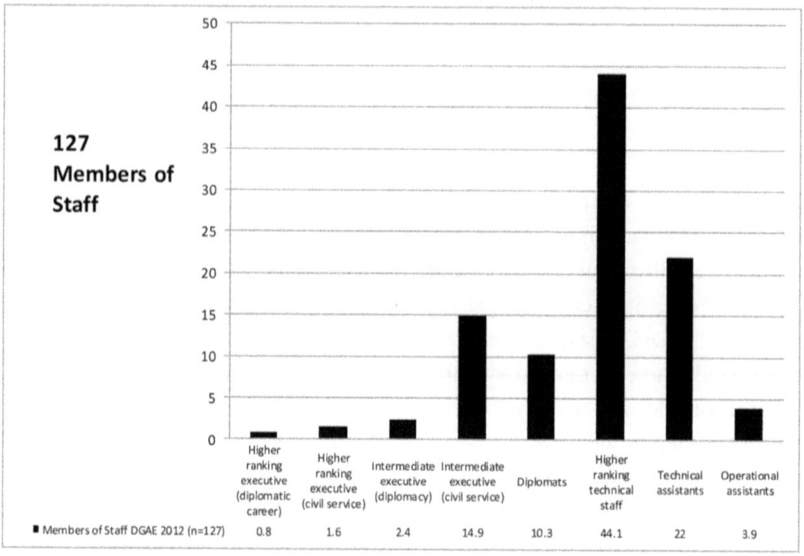

Figure 4.1 The composition of the General-Directorate for European Affairs according to hierarchical ranking (2012)

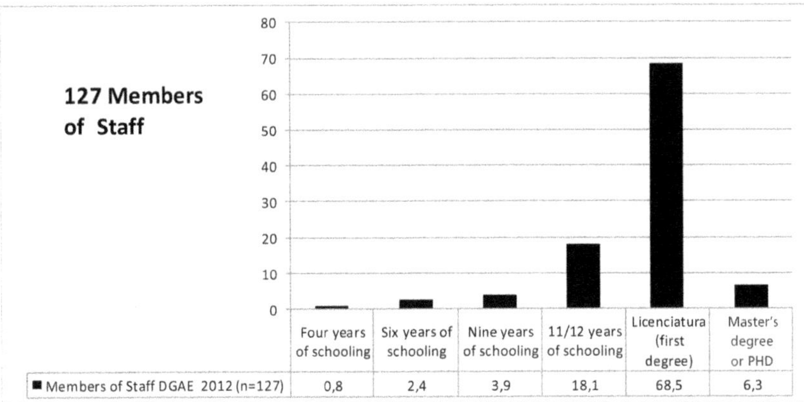

Figure 4.2 The qualification profile of the General-Directorate for European Affairs (2012)

European countries, mainly Greece, Italy, France, and Spain. Moreover, Maçães, who had completed his PhD in the United States, was quite pro-American, particularly in the negotiations of the Transatlantic Trade and Investment Partnership (TTIP), and he even went against the position of the European Commission (Jornal de Negócios, 24 September 2013).

At the core of the DGAE lies the Interministerial Commission of European Affairs (CIAE). Although it received a new statutory basis through decree-law 87/2012 of 10 April 2012 (which replaced former decree-law 345/91 of 17 September 1991 and 207/2007 of 29 May 2007), the whole structure remained untouched. Most of the changes were not about the purpose and objectives of the CIAE, but rather sought to improve the efficiency of this core coordinating structure. The CIAE is the main liaison structure with the Permanent Representation and is charged with defining the national position in relation to EU legislative proposals discussed in the working groups, the Committee of Permanent Representatives (COREPER) I and II, and the Article 126 Committee, which deals with the Common Trade Policy. The CIAE meets regularly at least once a month on Wednesday afternoons. It includes representatives of all ministries, normally at Secretary-of-State level with delegated powers from the ministers, and representatives from the autonomous regions of Madeira and Azores.

According to the decree-law, its main tasks are:

1. to analyse and debate the strategic questions of the EU and the presentation of the corresponding proposals according to the common orientation;

2. to deliberate on the issues that require interministerial coordination, thus defining national negotiating positions;
3. to secure the articulation of processes related to the European Semester;
4. to define national positions to be assumed in the different locations of European negotiation of the Multiannual Financing Framework;
5. to define the Portuguese orientation in pre-litigious and litigious matters of the EU;
6. to coordinate and monitor the transposition of EU legislation into national law; and
7. to examine, if necessary, matters relevant to the bilateral relationship of Portugal with the EU Member States, candidate countries, and countries of the EEA.

For specific purposes, for example in times before and during presidencies of the EU, the CIAE may create dedicated subcommittees, which may include more specialized civil servants and experts (see special issue by Cunha and Magone 2015).

The CIAE is an important reflective body to give guidance to the operational mission. In this respect, there is also a strong interest in upgrading the human and material resources to ensure that the Presidency is successful.

A second subcommittee that meets exceptionally every five to six years is related to the programming of structural/cohesion funds in the context of the Multiannual Financial Framework (MAFF). Portugal was quite successful in negotiating a total of about 20 billion Euros between 1988 and 2013. In addition, 21.5 billion Euros were allocated for the period 2010 to 2014, with a further 4.1 billion Euros destined for the agricultural sector from the European Fund for Rural Development.

Another central role of the CIAE is to facilitate the Portuguese position in the European Semester. The basic structure of the budget for the following year has to be ready before the summer. At the end of the process, the respective country will receive recommendations for further improvements of some financial aspects. Due to the bail-out programme, Portugal was excluded from the European Semester mechanism; immediately after the completion of the Troika regime in 2014–2015, it was integrated in the European Semester process for the first time. However, due to the national elections of 4 October 2015, in which no major party was able to win an absolute majority, the formation of a Government and approval by Parliament was difficult. Therefore, in spite of several requests by the European Commission to send the guiding data for the budget draft for 2015–2016, Portugal was only able to send it in January 2016. Following the negative opinion of the first scrutiny test by the European Commission, the new Socialist minority Government under Antonio

Costa had to make major changes. The very optimistic forecasts of the Government included in the budget were rejected by the European Commission outright; thus as expected additional measures were necessary in the second half of 2016 to achieve the agreed Growth and Stability Pact target of a 2.2 per cent budget deficit (Diário Económico, 5 February 2016; Jornal de Noticias, 5 February 2016).

4.2 The Permanent Representation: an excellent liaison structure

The success of national coordination of EU policy is highly dependent not only on the quality of the work of the DGAE but also on the Permanent Representation in Brussels (REPER). The REPER consists of the best civil servants Portugal has to offer. They are extremely well-trained, speak several languages, are experienced, and have a highly specialized knowledge of the workings of the EU. The vast majority of them were seconded by the ministries and report informally to them. Formally, however, their main addressees are the CIAE and the DGAE. The number of staff members has been growing steadily: in 1986, there were thirty-seven members of staff; in 1998, forty-seven; and in 2014, ninety-one including secretarial and supporting staff (Magone 2001, 173; the calculations for 2014 are based on information on the REPER website; see also Expresso, 18 July 2015). This shows how important it is for Portugal to have a good group of experts very close to the centres of EU decision-making. Normally, civil servants have the possibility to be seconded twice for a three-year period to international posts within the Portuguese administration. However, in 2012 a new law considerably restricted this possibility as well as the supplementary compensation subsidies, so that any civil servant interested in keeping this option had to sign a new contract consistent with the new rules. Many of them chose not to do so, therefore, when the law came into force in 2015, about twenty-eight positions in the Permanent Representation had to be replaced. By July 2015, the Government had replaced fourteen positions, which led to major criticism by the opposition. However, it seems that such changes are normal and tend to coincide with the change in political cycles (Expresso, 18 July 2015).

The Permanent Representatives are always extremely experienced diplomats because this post is one of the top positions in diplomacy. Some of the diplomats start out as Deputy Permanent Representatives before they later become Permanent Representatives in another round of diplomatic reshuffling. Permanent Representatives tend to stay for short periods of two to four years, while Deputy Permanent Representatives stay longer to ensure continuity. They are not political appointees and tend to be better integrated in the Brussels international and transEuropean community than in the national administrative one. During the Troika regime, the Permanent Representative was the diplomat Domingos Fezas Vital, who was appointed on 23 February 2011, which was during the Socrates Government. He then became the Ambassador to the United States, while his successor, Nuno Brito, moved to Brussels in October 2015, which was before the new Antonio Costa Government came to power. Both Fezas Vital and Nuno Brito had previously been Deputy Permanent Representatives in Brussels, and Nuno Brito had also been the Director General of DGAE.

The main task of the REPER is to protect national interests in the working group, COREPER, and Council of Ministers meetings. It is an important supporting structure for politicians flying out from Lisbon. Due to the considerable distance beween Lisbon and the centres of European decision-making, the REPER gains a special role in the national coordination of EU policy. It is the information-gathering machinery for all the ministries in Lisbon, particularly the CIAE and the DGAE. Turnover of staff has decreased over time since it is important for Portuguese civil service and diplomacy to have a stable structure at the forefront of European decision-making.

Due to their expertise and experience, most civil servants and diplomats are at a senior level. There is a strong culture of cooperation and teamwork in order to achieve the best results for the country in the decision-making bodies. There are just two levels, the higher ranking diplomats (Permanent Representative, Deputy Permanent Representative, and the Representative for the Political and Security Committee) and the expert civil servants. Therefore, a flat hierarchy dominates the REPER.

The REPER is a sophisticated machine that is well-adjusted to the European institutions in order to get the best information available regarding negotiation processes in the working committees, COREPER, and the Council of Ministers meetings. There is no strong ambition to play a central role in the arena of decision-making. On the contrary, research done by Jan Beyers and Guido Dierickx during the Belgian Presidency in 1998 shows that Portugal is a peripheral rather than a central actor in the EU. At the centre of decision-making are the big three, Germany, France, and the UK. Then there is a second group of small Northern European countries, Benelux, Ireland, and Denmark; a group that Finland, Sweden, and Austria joined in 1995. The third group comprises the Southern and, since 2004, Central and Eastern European countries; I would speculate that this is due to their weaker economies and dependency on EU funds. The crisis has certainly highlighted this division of centre and periphery in decision-making (on this divide: Beyers and Dierickx 1998, 305–306).

Although Portugal does not have the resources and power to be an agenda-setter or rule-maker, it sometimes punches above its weight when issues of national interest are at stake. The Permanent Representation steps up its efforts when it has to deal with the following issues:

1. the negotiations of the Multiannual Financial Framework (MAFF), particularly in relation to EU funding for the peripheral countries;
2. the negotiations with the European Commission concerning the common support framework, or, as it is now called, the Partnership Agreement;
3. the negotiations of new treaties in intergovernmental conferences, or in the Convention of Europe, particularly to ensure issues of national interest (e.g. adequate voting procedures for countries in the Council of Ministers);
4. the organization and running of the Presidency.

In all other issues, Portugal certainly looks for compromises that do not affect the Portuguese economy and society adversely.

The most important issue probably is negotiating the same level of funding that has been granted since 1988/1992, about 20 billion Euros. In this regard, Portugal has been proactive in keeping the cohesion group, which consists of Southern, Central, and Eastern European countries plus Ireland and Belgium, together. Before the rounds of negotiations, the Portuguese Permanent Representation engages in coordinating the positions of these countries' Representatives. This has clearly led to a considerable polarization between the net payer countries, particularly the UK, France, Germany, Austria, Sweden, the Netherlands, and Finland, also known as the 'Friends of Better Spending', against the so-called 'Friends of Cohesion'. The crisis has exacerbated this conflict due to the reduction of the 2014–2020 MAFF to 960 billion Euros. The Portuguese Government organized at least two informal meetings of coordination, one in Lisbon on 4 May 2012 and one in Brussels in the Permanent Representation on 13 November 2012 (Magone, Laffan and Schweiger 2016, 7). Portuguese diplomats have been quite successful in ensuring the same level of funding for the past two and a half decades. This is due to excellent expertise and cooperation between diplomats and civil servants in the REPER.

This was not the first time that Portugal had been proactive in shaping decision-making processes. Former Secretary of State of European Affairs, Francisco Seixas da Costa, recounted tales of meetings in the Permanent Representation of Member States of about 10 to 18 million people (like Portugal, Hungary, the Czech Republic, the Netherlands, and Belgium), which wanted to prevent any strengthening of the larger countries. Due to the poor outcome for these countries, the Nice European Council proved to be a bad experience for the Portuguese Government, particularly in relation to the weighting of the vote in the Council (Costa 2001, 61–68).

However, the Portuguese Government also learned to be more flexible in terms of alliances. Depending on the colour of government, we may see alliances with governments of the same party family. For example, the Passos Coelho Government formed a strong alliance with Germany because Portugal presented itself as a 'good pupil of the European Union' by fulfilling its homework given by the Troika. The successor Socialist minority Government, which is supported by a left-wing parliamentary majority that consists of socialists, communists, and the so-called 'block of the left' (*Bloco de Esquerda*), has sought alliances with left-wing governments in France, Italy, and Greece against the creditor countries in the Eurogroup rallying around Germany.

Like any other Permanent Representation, the Portuguese REPER tends to follow four generic patterns, recognized by Jeffrey Lewis (1998, 490–491):

> 1. *Departing from instructions and making recommendations:* In many cases, the instructions by the executive do not reflect the necessary approach to be taken in the negotiating process; the REPER may thus send recommendations to change the instructions. This seems to have increasingly become common practice, which has led to a – sometimes very informal – dialogue about the approach to take in a particular situation.
> 2. *The national capital signals that a margin of manoeuvre exists:* The expertise of the members of the REPER in negotiations and discussions gives them a special status in the coordination of EU policy. They are conferred with a margin of manoeuvre in order to achieve the best possible outcome for the Portuguese delegation.
> 3. *There is a political need to minimize confrontation:* For Portugal, the general approach is to be consensual. The avoidance of confrontation has been the general pattern in the Portuguese case. As a small State, the Portuguese public administration prefers to come to a compromise through REPER rather than to bring issues before the Council.
> 4. *The national capital cannot make up its mind:* The Government's distance to the negotiating arena and to the dynamics among different COREPER actors leads to a strengthening of the position of the REPER as the actual master of instructions. The reports received in Lisbon from REPER may come back to Brussels as instructions because the Portuguese CIAE trusts the expertise and knowledge of REPER.
>
> (Magone 2004, 156)

In this sense, Portuguese Permanent Representatives and civil servants at REPER are not very different from their counterparts in Brussels. Jonathan Aus characterized Permanent Representatives (*Ständige Vertreter*) as Permanent Traitors (*Ständige Verräter*) of the national interest because of their tendency to seek compromise in the transnational networks established around the various working groups in the Council of the EU.[1] These national representatives know each other very well and are therefore sometimes able to anticipate compromises that can be accepted in the capitals of all Member States.

4.3 The environment of national coordination of EU policy

The turning point for Portugal to assume a more assertive role came after the adoption of the Treaty of the European Union in 1993, which also included a protocol on the role of national parliaments in the European integration process. New law 20/94 of 15 June 1994 strengthened the process of scrutiny, in which the Committee of European Affairs became a central piece. It clearly had a coordinating role in relation to all committees and the climax was the critical review of the annual report prepared by the DGAC. The Committee of European Affairs was able to play an important role because the former Minister of Finance, Jorge Braga de Macedo, took over the chairmanship and worked hard to give salience to European issues in the national parliament (Magone 1995, 157). Between 1994 and 2006, the Committee of European Affairs was able to gain a good reputation and influence, in spite of the low level of human and material resources. However, the reporting of the Government was poor. The annual report was written in a legal language and lacked self-reflection and self-criticism. Finally, a new law in 2006 upgraded the role of Parliament in relation to the executive and European institutions. The new law gives *ex ante* powers of scrutiny to the Committee of European Affairs, which allows for a more active role in scrutinizing European legislative proposals (Resende and Paulo 2012; Janc˅ic˅, 2011). Among the Southern European parliaments, Portugal has certainly one of the strongest Parliaments along with Italy (Magone 2007a and 2007b).

In contrast, civil society has been rather sidelined in this process. There are certainly attempts at lobbying by major interest groups such as the Farmers' Confederation (CAP) and the Industry Confederation (CIP); however, this is limited due to the low level of influence on Portuguese representatives in Brussels.

5 The sovereign debt crisis and the Troika: coordinating the Economic and Financial Adjustment Programme (2011–2014)

A major burden for Portuguese public administration was the coordination of the Economic and Financial Adjustment Programme agreed upon with the Troika on 5 May 2011 and signed on 17 May 2011. Although DGAE and REPER were important sources of information and support, most of the work related to national economic policy was undertaken by the Office of the PM and the MF.

After the sovereign debt crisis in Greece in 2010, all other countries in the Eurozone began to be scrutinized more closely by rating agencies. The Southern European countries, including France, were more in the spotlight of the largely unstable markets after the housing bubble burst in the United States in 2008–2009. Many countries, including Portugal, bailed out national banks, which led to an increase in the budget deficit to above 3 per cent of GDP and in the public-debt ratio to above 60 per cent of GDP. Greece successfully asked for a bail-out, but this was made conditional on a package of conjunctural and structural measures. Despite the difficulty in adhering to the strict requirements, a second bail-out was agreed upon in 2011 (for more detail, see Visvizi 2014). At the end of 2010, Ireland also asked for a bail-out. In the meantime, the EU had created a large bail-out fund, the European Financial Stability Fund (EFSF), to which Member States could apply; in 2012, this was transformed into a permanent European Stability Mechanism (ESM). Moreover, a smaller fund was established by the European Commission; however, it was always attached to strict conditions. The whole process was rather improvised and a direct consequence of market pressures. Since the Lisbon Treaty forbade any bail-out, the whole process was developed parallel to the actual treaties as an intergovernmental process. This meant that bail-outs had not only to be agreed upon between the Eurozone members but that each Member State had to get approval from its national Parliament. Germany had the largest share of the burden with about 28 per cent. Therefore, Chancellor Angela Merkel was very keen to get the International Monetary Fund (IMF) on board in order to prevent European institutions (the European Commission and the European Central Bank [ECB]) from being too soft on these countries. One of the reasons may have been that Southern Europeans were in charge of these institutions: the Portuguese José Manuel Durão Barroso as President of the European Commission and the Italian Mario Draghi as President of the ECB. Therefore, a so-called Troika, which consisted of the European Commission, the ECB, and the IMF, was established to manage these issues effectively. PM José Socrates, who was in charge of the Socialist minority Government after the September elections of 2009, had to deal with a rather hostile Parliament after four years of absolute-majority government. This complex environment was certainly one of the factors leading up to the political and economic crisis in Portugal (for more detail, see Magone 2013; Magone et al. 2016, 6–9).

PM Socrates tried to resist until the end of March 2011, when the fourth major package of austerity measures was rejected by all political parties of the opposition. He resigned on 23 March 2011, and new early elections were announced later by the President after consultation with the advisory

State Council. In spite of being a caretaker government, the President of the Republic, Anibal Cavaco Silva, the other political parties, the banking sector, and even his own party forced Socrates to negotiate the programme (for an excellent account based on detailed research, see Dinis and Coelho 2012). As in the cases of Greece and Ireland, an extensive programme of conjunctural and structural reforms was drafted. The second largest party, the Social Democrats (PSD), and the Democratic Social Centre-People's Party (CDS-PP) were supportive of the programme and committed themselves to implementing it should they come out as winners of the elections on 5 June 2011. Only the left-wing Communist Party (*Partido Comunista Português*) and the so-called 'block of the left' (*Bloco da Esquerda*) decided not to support the programme or even talk to the Troika negotiators.

The elections on 5 June 2011 led to the victory of the conservative Social Democrats, who formed a coalition with the CDS-PP. The coalition agreement focused on the implementation of the Memorandum of Understanding (MoU). Both parties regarded the bail-out conditions as a loss of socio-economic sovereignty. Therefore, the main target was to implement the reforms and complete the programme successfully, so that economic sovereignty could be regained.

Therefore, a temporary taskforce was created to coordinate the implementation of the programme. It was called the Mission of Monitoring the Memoranda (*Missão de Acompanhamento dos Memorandums*, ESAME) and started work in July 2011, two weeks after the Government was officially in place. The ESAME was located in São Bento, close to the Office of the PM. A Secretary of State to the PM, Carlos Moedas, was in charge of chairing this temporary taskforce, which would be dissolved once the programme had been successfully implemented. This was scheduled for 30 June 2014. The aim was to achieve the highest level of efficiency in the implementation of the vast programme of measures. According to the official final report, over 450 measures were implemented by the Government in 1,000 days (Governo de Portugal 2014b, 10).

Another important aim was to avoid too much delay in the transition from the previous to the new Government. Clearly, some of the measures had to be implemented following tight guidelines in order to obtain a positive assessment at the Troika review, which was necessary to get the respective payment. In total, Portugal had twelve such Troika visits between July 2011 and May 2014 (Table 4.2). These were quite serious negotiation meetings with very well-prepared officials from the European Commission, the European Central Bank (ECB), and the International Monetary Fund (IMF) (Governo de Portugal 2014b, 12).

Carlos Moedas had already been a negotiator of the programme with the Troika, which meant that his leadership now endowed the whole process with

Table 4.2 The twelve visits of the Troika (2011–2014)

Reviews	*Date*
Memorandum of Understanding	17 May 2011
First Review	1 September 2011
Second Review	9 December 2011
Third Review	15 March 2012
Fourth Review	27 March 2012
Fifth Review	14 October 2012
Sixth Review	19 December 2012
Seventh Review	12 June 2013
Eighth and Ninth Review	24 October 2013
Tenth Review	27 January 2014
Eleventh Review	28 March 2014
Twelfth Review	1 May 2014

Table 4.3 Portugal's Adjustment Programme negotiated with the Troika (2011–2014)

AREA	**OBJECTIVE**
SHORT-TERM MEASURES	
FISCAL POLICIES	
Budget deficit reduction	From 9.5 percent of GDP to below 3 percent in 2013 (2014)
	Streamlining of budgetary framework and use of strategic management to overview expenditure
Internal debt commitments	Control, transparency, and speedy payment of debt obligations to the private sector by the State
FINANCIAL SECTOR	
Banking sector	Upgrade and reform of regulation and supervision; bank crisis as important factor in budget deficit
MEDIUM-TERM REFORMS AND MEASURES	
MARKET DE-REGULATION	
Liberalization of markets for goods and services	• Energy markets • Telecommunications and postal services • Transport and other service sectors • Housing market
Business culture	• Improvement of competition mechanisms • Improvement of public procurement • Improvement of business environment
Labor-market reform	• Improved flexibility in the labor market • Reform of unemployment benefits • Measures against long-term unemployment • Reduction in severance costs (from 20 to 12 days per year of work as compensation) • Wage reform • Active labor-market policies

AREA	OBJECTIVE
NATIONAL HEALTH SERVICE	
Pharmaceuticals	• Monitoring and reduction of debt to the pharmaceutical industry • Cheaper online purchase of pharmaceuticals
PUBLIC ECONOMIC SECTOR	
Public-private partnerships	Review of public-private partnerships and freezing of new contracts
Public-enterprise sector	Improvements in governance of the public-enterprise sector • Reduction in subsidies • Managerial best practices (according to international standards) • Debt ceilings • Privatization ○ Portuguese airlines (TAP) ○ main electricity company (EDP) ○ airport management (ANA) ○ oil company (GALP) ○ energy company (REN) ○ postal service (Correios de Portugal) ○ freight branch of national railways ○ insurance company (Caixa Seguros) ○ nationalized bank (BPN)
LONG-TERM REFORMS	
STATE REFORM	
Taxation administration	Streamlining and unification of revenue administration through the merging of various existing units
Central public administration reform	• Leaner public administration ○ reduction of top executive positions ○ non-replacement of retiring civil servants ○ streamlining accounting at the regional and local levels ○ continuation of reduction in services and administrative units ○ enhanced flexibility and mobility of human resources
Local government reform	• Reduction in parishes (new local government map) • Introduction of new public-management philosophy • New electoral law • Reduction in number of elected offices • Reform of the local public-enterprise sector (reduction in enterprises)
JUDICIARY	
Reform of the judiciary sector	• New judiciary map • Introduction of new managerial philosophy in the micro-court system
EDUCATION AND TRAINING	
Education	Reduction of number of school leavers in the secondary education
Training	Improvement of vocational training

Sources: European Commission, European Central Bank, International Monetary Fund 2011; Magone 2014b.

continuity. The ESAME consisted of a small team of ten to fifteen people. Although it had the possibility to expand to thirty people, it remained small and flexible throughout the period. It liaised with correspondents in the ministries concerned so that the flow of information and instructions could be maintained. Moreover, it was the ESAME that arranged the visits and kept the channels of communications with the Troika open. Last but not least, the ESAME also had an informational task at the international level (Governo de Portugal 2014b, 12; see Figure 4.3).

The ESAME worked closely with the PM and the Minister of Finance. While the PM remained an important element of stability, the resignation of the Minister of Finance Vitor Gaspar at the end of June 2013 created major uncertainty. This was exacerbated when the leader of the junior coalition partner, Paulo Portas, resigned over the appointment of Maria Luis Albuquerque as new Minister of Finance. The position of the Minister of Finance is a powerful position, and Paulo Portas felt passed over. However, after negotiations between the two parties, it was finally agreed that Paulo Portas would become Vice-PM and be in charge of economic coordination. In this sense, this position put him hierarchically above the new Minister of Finance. This political crisis had a positive effect on coordination because the situation improved after this reshuffle. Minister of Finance Albuquerque gained a considerable reputation among the Troika due to her expertise (Magone 2014b, 355).

The ESAME also had to report to Parliament. A dedicated *ad hoc* body was set up to oversee this process. The work of the so-called 'Eventual Commission to Accompany the Measures of the Financial-Assistance Programme to

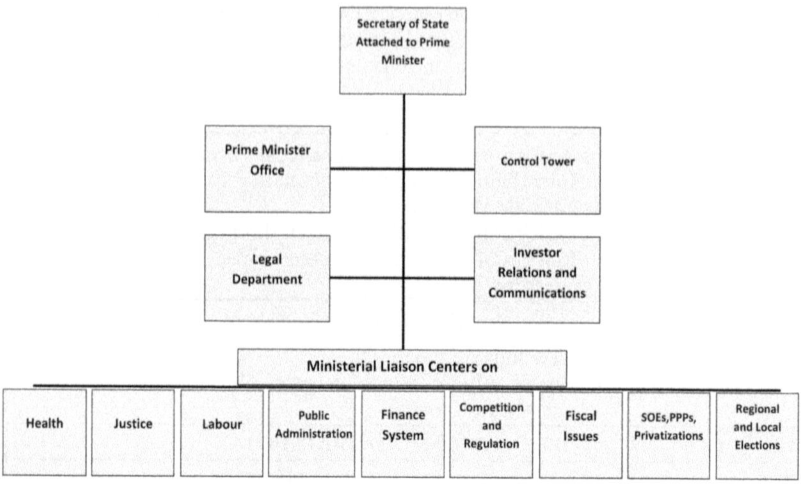

Figure 4.3 The monitoring unit of the Economic and Financial Adjustment Programme (ESAME)

Portugal' (*Comissão Eventual para Acompanhamento das Medidas do Programa de Assistência Financeira a Portugal*) started on 6 July 2011.

The Troika also paid visits to Parliament. The aforementioned Eventual Commission was the main structure accommodating this intensified relationship with the Troika. In total, there were forty-five meetings, thirty-eight auditions with the representatives of the Troika, members of Government and interest groups, and six audiences with other external actors, such as the European Parliament. Clearly, Parliament was largely informed about progress made. Apart from this, there were six audiences with other institutions, including a group of representatives of the German Christian Social Union (*Christlich-Soziale Union*, CSU) from the Bavarian Parliament on 29 December 2012 (Assembleia da República 2014; Público 24 May 2012).

6 Conclusion

In spite of the difficulties that emerged from the economic and financial crisis, the basic structure of the Portuguese coordination of EU policy did not change very much. Although new legislation amended the role of the DGAE in the policy-making process, particularly by adding economic coordination in relation to the European Semester, everything else remained the same. One can observe a drive to make the whole process more efficient and to create better value for money. People recruited to the DGAE or the REPER are extremely experienced and well trained. These diplomats and civil servants speak several languages and those in the REPER are excellent negotiators. The crisis did not negatively affect any of this. The sovereign debt crisis led to innovative new forms of coordination, such as ESAME, outside of the traditional structures. The package of reforms was looked at in a positive way. Instead of looking at them with suspicion, the reforms were implemented professionally and in cooperation with the institutions. Accountability and transparency became important aspects. In this sense, the loss of financial sovereignty may have triggered a new mentality among policy-makers. It was a learning curve experienced under stress in order to come out of the programme with a changed, slimmer, and more efficient State. The only question that remains in the future is whether the dynamics of the past three years will be continued or whether previous paternalistic patterns of behaviour may return and reduce the impact of the reforms.

Note

1 According to Jonathan Aus, this was expressed half-jokingly by the long-standing German Permanent Representative Dietrich von Kyauw, who worked in Brussels between 1993 and 1999 (Aus 2006, 11).

Bibliography

Assembleia da República (2014) 'Comissão Eventual para Acompanhamento das Medidas do Programa de Assistência Financeira a Portugal', http://www.parlamento.pt/sites/com/XIILeg/CEAMPAFP/Paginas/default.aspx.

Aus J. (2006) *Logics of Decision-Making on Community Asylum-Policy. A Case Study of Evolvement of the Dublin II Regulation*, Oslo, Centre of European Studies. Arena, University of Oslo Working Paper 3, February.

Beyers J. and Dierickx, G. (1998) 'The Working Groups of the Council of the European Union: Supranational or Intergovernmental Negotiations?', *Journal of Common Market Studies* 36 (3) (289–317).

Börzel T. (2005) 'Europeanization: How the European Union Interacts with Its Member States', in Bulmer S. and Lequesne C. (eds.), *The Member States of the European Union*, Oxford, Oxford University Press (25–44).

Conselho de Ministros (2006) *Resolution Nr. 4*, 29 December 1985 (approval of temporary mission structure for preparation of the Presidency).

Correia J. (2006) 'A Integração na União Europeia e o Papel do Ministério dos Negócios Estrangeiros', *Nação e Defesa* 115 (29–81).

Costa F. (2001) 'Portugal e o Tratado de Nice: Notas sobre a estratégia negocial portuguesa', *Negócios Estrangeiros* 1 (40–70).

Cunha A. and Magone J. (2015) (eds.) *The Iberian Presidencies of the European Union. Between Ambition and the Constraints of the Reality*, Special Issue of *International Journal of Iberian Studies* 28 (2–3).

Diário da República (DR) (1985a), Ministério dos Negócios Estrangeiros, decree-law 459/85, I. Série, Nr. 253, 4 November 1985 (3698–3699) (Permanent Representation to the European Communities, REPER).

Diário da República (DR) (1985b), Ministério dos Negócios Estrangeiros, decree-law 527/85, I. Série, Nr. 301, 31 December 1985, 4260 (134) (Interministerial Commission of the European Communities, CICE).

Diário da República (DR) (1991), Ministério dos Negócios Estrangeiros, decree-law 354/91, I. Série, Nr. 214, 17 September 1991 (4908) (updated version of Interministerial Commission of European Communities, CICE).

Diário da República (DR) (1994), Ministério dos Negócios Estrangeiros, decree-law 49/94, I. Série A, Nr. 46, 24 February 1994 (830–8358) (Directorate General of Community Affairs, DGAC).

Diário da República (DR) (2006), Ministério dos Negócios Estrangeiros, decree-law 204/2006, I. Série, Nr. 208, 27 October 2006 (7447–7454) (Directorate-General for European Affairs, DGAE).

Diário da República (DR) (2007), Ministério dos Negócios Estrangeiros, decree-law 207/2007, I. Série, Nr. 103, 29 May 2007 (3460–3462) (Interministerial Commission of European Affairs, CIAE).

Diário da República (DR) (2012), Ministério dos Negócios Estrangeiros, decree-law 87/2012, I. Série, Nr. 71, 10 April 2012 (1785).

Diario de Noticias (5 April 2011.) 'Reestruturação da Administração Central Estado suspensa, diz o governo', http://www.dn.pt/economia/interior/reestruturacao-da-administracao-central-estado-suspensa-diz-o-governo--1823458.html.

Diário Económico (5 February 2016) 'Bruxelas aprova orçamento mas deixa recados a Costa', http://economico.sapo.pt/noticias/bruxelas-aprova-orcamento-mas-deixa-recados-a-costa_241854.html.

Dinis D. and Coelho H. (2012) *Resgatados. Os Bastidores da Ajuda Financeira a Portugal*, Lisbon, A Esfera dos Livros.

Direcção Geral de Assuntos Europeus (DGAE) (2012) *Relatório de Actividades 2011.*

Direcção Geral de Assuntos Europeus (DGAE) (2013) *Relatório de Actividades 2012.*

European Commission, European Central Bank, International Monetary Fund (2011) *Memorandum of Understanding on Specific Economic Conditionality*, http://economico.sapo.pt/public/uploads/memorando_04–05–2011.pdf.

Expresso (18 July 2015) 'Governo nomeia leva de técnicos para a Reper', http://expresso.sapo.pt/politica/2015-07-18-Governo-nomeia-leva-de-tecnicos-para--a-Reper.

Governo de Portugal (2011) 'Economic and Financial Adjustment Programme', First Quarterly Review, ESAME-Monitoring Unit for the Implementation for the Economic and Financial Adjustment Programme, 3 September 2011, PowerPoint presentation, http://www.portugal.gov.pt/media/371896/ir_1r_pres_results_110905.pdf.

Governo de Portugal (2012) *Plano de Redução e Melhoria da Administração Central. Relatório Final de Aplicação*, Lisbon, Governo de Portugal.

Governo de Portugal (2014a) Database on governments, http://www.portugal.gov.pt/pt/o-governo/arquivo-historico.aspx.

Governo de Portugal (2014b) *A Gestão do Programa de Ajustamento. 1000 dias and 450 medidas cumpridas*, http://www.portugal.gov.pt/media/1413075/20140508%20seapm%20gestao%20paef.pdf.

Jančić D. (2011) 'The Portuguese Parliament: Blazing the Trail to the European Scrutiny Trophy', *Interdisciplinary Political Studies* 1 (1) (93–108).

Jančić D. (2014) 'The Portuguese Parliament and EU Affairs: From Inert to Agile Democratic Control', in Hefftler C., Neuhold C., Rozenberg O. and Smith J. (eds.), *Palgrave Handbook on National Parliaments in the European Union*, Basingstroke, Palgrave (366–86).

Jornal de Negócios (24 September 2013) 'Bruno Maçães: "Portugal tem muito a ganhar com maior integração europeia"', http://www.jornaldenegocios.pt/economia/europa/uniao_europeia/zona_euro/detalhe/bruno_macaes_portugal_tem_muito_a_ganhar_de_uma_maior_integracao_europeia.html.

Jornal de Notícias (5 February 2016) 'Bruxelas aprovou esboço de orçamento para 2016', http://www.jn.pt/economia/interior/bruxelas-aprovou-orcamento-2016-5016878.html.

Kassim H. (2015) 'Patterns of National Coordination of EU Policy', in Magone J. (ed.), *Routledge Handbook of European Politics*, London, Routledge (686–707).

Leston-Bandeira C. (2004) *From Legislation to Legitimation. The Role of the Portuguese Parliament*, London, Routledge.

Lewis J. (1998) 'Is the "Hard Bargaining" Image of the Council Misleading? The Committee of Permanent Representatives and the Local Elections Directive', *Journal of Common Market Studies* 36 (4) (479–504).

Luis F. (2014) *Crónica de um Resgate Anunciado. A história e os bastidores da intervenção. Os países de um país sem Troika*, Lisbon, Clube de Autor.

Magone J. (1995) 'The Portuguese Assembleia da República: Discovering Europe', *Journal of Legislative Studies* 1 (3) (151–167).

Magone J. (2000) 'Portugal', in Kassim H., Peters B.G. and Wright V. (eds.), *The National Co-ordination of EU Policy. The Domestic Level*, Oxford, Oxford University Press (141–160).

Magone J. (2001) 'The Portuguese Permanent Representation in Brussels: The Institutionalization of a Simple System', in Kassim H., Peters B.G. and Wright V. (eds.), *The National Co-ordination of EU Policy. The European Level*, Oxford, Oxford University Press (168–190).

Magone J. (2004) *The Developing Place of Portugal in the European Union*, New Brunswick, NJ, Transaction.

Magone J. (2007a) 'The Southern European Pattern of Parliamentary Scrutiny of EU Legislation: Emulating the French Model', in Holzhacker R. and Albaek E. (eds.), *Democratic Governance and European Integration. Linking Societal and State Processes of Democracy*, Cheltenham, Edward and Elgar (229–248).

Magone J. (2007b) 'Southern European National Parliaments and the European Union. An Inconsistent Reactive Revival', in O'Brennan J. and Raunio T. (eds.), *National Parliaments within the European Union. From 'Victims' of Integration to Competitive Actors?*, London, Routledge (116–131).

Magone J. (2011a) 'The Difficult Transformation of State and Public Administration in Portugal. Europeanization and the Persistence of Neo-Patrimonialism', *Public Administration* 89 (3) (756–782).

Magone J. (2011b) 'Centre-Periphery Conflict in the European Union? Europe 2020, the Southern European Model and the Euro-Crisis', in Ágh A. (ed.), *European Union at the Crossroads. The European Perspectives after the Global Crisis*, Budapest, Budapest College of Communication, Business and Arts (60–112).

Magone J. (2013) 'Living with the Crisis in Southern Europe', in Ágh A. and Voss L. (eds.), *European Futures: The Perspectives of the New Member-States in the New Europe*, Budapest, Budapest College of Communication, Business and Arts (69–112).

Magone J. (2014a) *The Politics in Contemporary Portugal. Evolving Democracy*, Boulder, CO, Lynne Rienner.

Magone J. (2014b) 'Portugal is not Greece: Policy Responses in the Sovereign Debt Crisis and the Consequences for the Portuguese Political Economy', *Perspectives on European Politics and Society* 15 (3) (346–360).

Magone J. (2016) 'Portugal as the "Good Pupil of the European Union". Living under the Regime of the Troika', in Magone J., Laffan B. and Schweiger C. (eds.), *Core-Periphery Relations in the European Union. Power and Conflict in a Dualist Political Economy*, London, Routledge (179–189).

Magone J., Laffan B., and Schweiger C. (2016) 'The European Union as a Dualist Political Economy. Understanding Core-Periphery Relations', in Magone J., Laffan B. and Schweiger C. (eds.), *Core-Periphery Relations in the European Union. Power and Conflict in a Dualist Political Economy*, London, Routledge (1–16).

Público (24 May 2012) 'Troika acredita que "abrandamento da recessão" já está em curso', https://www.publico.pt/economia/noticia/troika-acredita-que-abrandamento-da-recessao-ja-esta-em-curso-1547489.

Resende M.M. and Paulo M.T. (2012) 'Implementing the Treaty of Lisbon: The Portuguese Parliament as an Actor in the European Legislative Arena', in Teixeira N.S. and Costa Pinto A. (eds.), *The Europeanization of Portuguese Democracy*, New York, Columbia University Press (85–109).

Sol (17 December 2013) 'Aliança do Sul contra o Norte da Europa é Ideia do Século XIX', http://sol.sapo.pt/noticia/95010/alian%C3%A7a-do-sul-contra-o-norte-da-europa-%C3%A9-ideia-do-s%C3%A9c-xix.

Torres F. (1998) 'The Case for Economic and Monetary Union: Europe and Portugal', *Nação e Defesa* 85 (2) (29–69).

Torres F. (2000) 'Lessons from Portugal's Long Transition to Economic and Monetary Union', in de Vasconcelos A. and Seabra M.J. (eds.), *Portugal. A European Story*, Lisbon, Principia (99–130).

Torres F. (2009) 'Policy Responses to the Financial Crisis in the Eurozone: The Case of Portugal', *South European Society and Politics* 14 (1) (55–70).

Visvizi A. (2014) 'From Grexit to Grecovery: The Paradox of the Troika's Engagement with Greece', *Perspectives in European Politics and Society* 15 (3) (335–345).

5 EU coordination in Cyprus

The limits of Europeanization in times of crisis

Adonis Pegasiou

1 Introduction

Despite being a European Union (EU) member for more than a decade, Cyprus has not yet established an effective and permanent coordination mechanism for European affairs, rendering the country an outlier within the EU. Any attempts to set up such a mechanism have been made on an *ad hoc* basis, initially to coordinate the negotiations for accession into the EU and later to better manage the country's Presidency of the EU Council in the second semester of 2012. Domestic blockages and interinstitutional rivalry at the national level did not allow such temporary institutional arrangements to evolve into something permanent, despite acknowledgement at the highest political level of the necessity for such a mechanism in order to facilitate Cyprus' EU membership.

As a result, when the country requested international financial assistance in June 2012, there was no existing permanent structure that could coordinate the negotiations between the Cypriot Government and the Troika (International Monetary Fund [IMF], European Central Bank [ECB], and European Commission) and, consequently, *ad hoc* arrangements were once again pursued. The existence of such a mechanism would have possibly enabled a better management of the negotiations over the financial assistance programme and could have helped avoid a delay in the final agreement.

With the change in Government in February 2013, following the election of right-wing Nicos Anastasiades as President, and the signing of the Memorandum of Understanding (MoU) shortly thereafter, the newly appointed Minister of Finance was given *carte blanche* in overseeing all communication and interaction with the Troika. In addition, the technocrats of the Ministry of Finance (MF), previously in a simmering struggle with the left-wing Government due to underlying conflicting ideologies, have been more aligned with the Government's objectives and have been utilized accordingly, securing a smooth coordination of the implementation of the programme.

It is essential to note that, parallel to the efforts to successfully manage the implementation of the financial assistance programme, the Ministry of Foreign Affairs (MFA) proposed the creation of a coordination mechanism for EU affairs under the MFA, which the Government accepted in December 2013. Nevertheless, the establishment of such a mechanism has, in practice, once more proven a futile initiative.

The aim of this chapter is to initially examine why attempts to create a permanent coordination mechanism have proven unsuccessful to date and, in addition, to see how the present Government has managed to secure to a large extent the timely implementation of the MoU within the agreed three-year timeframe. In doing so, the chapter begins with the political and institutional setting in Cyprus and investigates how the unresolved national problem has allowed for particular characteristics to develop that have influenced the structure of the civil service and the framework within which successive Governments have functioned. The following section seeks to shed light on two periods, namely the period of EU accession negotiations and that of the Presidency of the EU Council, since both are considered to be 'critical junctures' for the creation of an EU affairs coordination mechanism. In these two periods, the Governments in office acted rationally and pursued the establishment of such a mechanism, albeit within a fixed timeframe and on a temporary basis. The chapter then reviews the request for, agreement to, and execution of the MoU, and the roles assigned to existing institutions for the negotiation, coordination, and implementation of the relevant MoU requirements. The financial assistance package is not considered a critical juncture for the formation of an EU affairs coordination mechanism, as the two were never linked in any way, though other significant institutional reforms resulted from this period. Finally, reference is made to the latest, unsuccessful attempt of the Government to set an EU affairs coordination mechanism within the MFA.

In explaining how relevant developments evolved, the chapter makes use of new institutionalism theory, juxtaposing all three of the new institutionalist approaches and utilizing them in a complementary way. A rational approach is more appropriate and functional to account for the creation of temporary coordination mechanisms during the aforementioned critical junctures. In assessing why these structures did not turn into something permanent, this chapter argues that path-dependent and strongly embedded mentalities within State institutions proved to be the decisive factors. Any possible alternative to the path followed historically could challenge the authority enjoyed by the established institutions which would not easily consent to such a possibility. The prevalence of such traditional modes of functioning, which essentially deprived coordination mechanisms from being sustainable, is better explained through a cultural/sociological prism and the associated 'thickness' of the existing institutions that favour the *status quo* (Checkel 1999).

To allow for such a nuanced understanding in which each of the three new-institutionalism approaches can explain different aspects of the puzzle, the framework of analysis: (i) traces historically (since accession negotiations commenced in 1998) how the relevant actors have reacted to the need to have a permanent coordination mechanism, with special reference to the periods considered as critical junctures; (ii) explores the capacity of the relevant actors in influencing developments in the domestic arena; and (iii) looks specifically at the era of the financial crisis and how this may have influenced the intragovernmental institutional balance of power. This approach helps reveal the complementarity of the three new-institutionalism strands and enables a better understanding of the case examined.

Furthermore, the chapter seeks to assess whether Cyprus' categorization according to Kassim's proposed grouping of EU policy coordination mechanisms is accurate. Kassim (2015) highlights the importance of taking into account at least two dimensions when classifying these national mechanisms: the first dimension refers to the ambition that underlies and informs the systems of coordination, with the most ambitious countries being those that wish to actively engage in all policy fronts open at the European level, in contrast to those countries that seek a more selective approach, focusing instead on those issues that are of direct national interest; the second dimension is the degree to which decision-making is concentrated. At one end of the spectrum, one finds highly centralized systems with ultimate authority resting in a single ministry or office, while at the other end there are countries with decentralized systems in which power is more evenly shared. The aim is to see whether Cyprus is correctly listed as a country with relatively limited ambition and a decentralized system.

2 The political and institutional setting of Cyprus

2.1 The birth and early history of the Republic of Cyprus

The Republic of Cyprus (RoC) is a relatively new regime, dating back to 1960, when it declared its independence after more than seventy years of British rule, the last imperial force of many that had ruled the island. The new constitution allowed for a unitary State to be governed by both communities, the Greek-Cypriots (G/Cs), which comprised around 80 per cent of the population, and the Turkish-Cypriots (T/Cs), which made up not more than 20 per cent of the population. Executive power was vested primarily in the hands of the President, who has since served as head of both State and Government. The post of

President was agreed to be filled by a Greek Cypriot while the main check on presidential power came from the Vice President, a position to be held by a T/C (Ker-Lindsay 2006 and 2008).

Following an attempt by President Makarios to introduce certain constitutional changes in December 1963, the T/Cs withdrew from Government, while a series of intercommunal clashes occurred in the following months.[1] A feeling of mistrust between the two communities continued to prevail in the years following the events of 1963–1964 and incidents of violence came to a head in 1974. On 15 July 1974, a *coup d'état* against President Makarios by far right G/C paramilitaries backed by the Greek Junta was followed by the Turkish invasion of 20 July 1974, which resulted in the illegal occupation by Turkish troops of Cyprus' northern part. The *de facto* division of the island has remained the paramount national issue for successive Cypriot Governments, dominating the agenda of all elected Presidents.

In the resulting political and institutional setting and given the empty post of Vice President, subsequent Presidents have performed their duties with limited checks and balances. The unquestionable authority of the President has been reinforced by the minimal powers of the House of Representatives to limit his actions, both in terms of the constitutional system in place and in terms of practical politics. At the same time, the President is also regarded by G/Cs as the national leader, in both a historical and cultural sense, since the presidential post has been assigned the task of leading all efforts towards finding a peaceful settlement to the 'Cyprus problem'. Effectively, at least within the EU, the President of Cyprus exerts more influence over his State than any other leader (Ker-Lindsay 2006).

2.2 *The rigid institutional framework of Cyprus*

The unresolved national issue and the constitutional rigidities arising from the non-participation of T/Cs in government have inevitably shaped the domestic institutional and political setting. The absence of T/Cs could potentially have halted the functioning of the government, which was avoided by the 'Doctrine of Necessity', while any possible revisions of the 1960 constitution would be legally complex if not impossible.[2]

The 1960 constitution clearly defined the number of ministries and ministers (ten in total) and that regulation was maintained, with the exception of adding the Ministry of Education. In 1985, the Supreme Court, following a request by then President Spyros Kyprianou, issued an opinion in which it reconfirmed that there were ten ministers and ministries of the Government of the RoC and that the President had no power to appoint more ministers (including deputy-ministers) or to create more than ten ministries (Supreme Court of Justice

1985). Any reform would be limited to changing the name of one of the existing ministries. This opinion has not been challenged since then, though some legal experts point out that a revision of this opinion could have been obtained if pursued.

It is, therefore, important to note that the applicable legal framework fostered permanent ministerial structures, which, over time, have allowed for the accumulation of competencies and authority for each ministry in a clearly path-dependent process. As a result, even if the legal barriers were to be lifted at some point, it would be difficult to overturn a deeply entrenched ministerial setting and a relevant culture that has been cultivated over the years with the creation of new ministries and/or other government services or the appointment of additional ministers and/or other political appointments that could essentially challenge the authority enjoyed by the existing ministries and the relevant high-ranking civil servants.

Overall, it is helpful to consider that the Cypriot civil-service model is close to the British one and thus draws on certain principles of the Weberian model of bureaucracy including neutrality, technical expertise, and permanence (Richards and Smith 2000). In such a bureaucratic model, Weber acknowledges the possibility of the bureaucrats (civil servants) evolving into an independent force in society with an inherent tendency to overstep their proper function as a technical instrument of politicians and to promote their set of interests, even if these contradict those of the elected Government (Dowding 1995, 106). It is therefore crucial to bear in mind that departments or groups within the Cypriot civil service could have turned into an independent force with the potential of shaping developments.

It is also worth noting that given the paramount importance that the unresolved national problem has for all Cypriots, the MFA has gained added status and authority through its crucial role in providing support to the President in the intercommunal talks aiming for a peace settlement. Confirming the enhanced role of the MFA, the Diplomatic Office established at the Presidency since 2003 is mainly headed and staffed by career diplomats.[3] As a result, although the constitution does not provide for any sort of hierarchical categorization between the ministries, the Cypriot MFA has assumed a more prominent role relative to the other ministries.

Apart from the institutional and political effects, the 'Cyprus problem' has also created a feeling of insecurity within society related to the illegal presence of Turkish troops in the northern occupied areas. Failure to reach a solution that would provide for the removal of all foreign troops prompted G/C political parties to unanimously and eagerly pursue EU accession as a source of security and protection, while some even considered that such a development could bring a new momentum to the peace talks.

3 Attempts to introduce an EU affairs coordination mechanism

This section aims to investigate the two critical junctures of the past two decades that required setting up an EU related coordination mechanism that could potentially have evolved into a permanent institutional structure. The term 'critical juncture' is derived from the historical strand of 'new institutionalism theory' and is taken to be a brief phase of institutional flux during which dramatic changes, with a possible lasting impact, are possible (Capoccia and Kelemen 2007). Critical junctures, therefore, can constitute a starting point for many path-dependent processes where institutions become persistent features of the historical landscape and central factors pushing historical development along a set of paths (Hall and Taylor 1996).

3.1 The road to EU accession – the first critical juncture

On 6 March 1995, the General Affairs Council reaffirmed the suitability of Cyprus for EU accession and in October 1996 the then Minister of Foreign Affairs Alekos Michaelides, a competent diplomat and negotiator, convinced President Glafcos Clerides to assign the responsibility of accession negotiations to the MFA. This arrangement proved to be complicated and rather ineffective since it involved the transfer of officials from the Planning Bureau[4] to the MFA. With the appointment of a new Minister of Foreign Affairs, Ioannis Kasoulides, in April 1997, there was an effort to reorganize the coordination mechanism for EU accession negotiations and Kasoulides was convinced of the need to transfer this unit to the Planning Bureau.

Following his re-election in February 1998, President Clerides decided that a political appointment was necessary to lead accession negotiations, set to start in March 1998, and to head the relevant team of civil servants from the Planning Bureau. Former President Vassiliou, a respected and dedicated pro-European politician, was thus selected for the position of Head of the Accession Negotiations (Council of Ministers – CoM – Decision 47.496, 6 March 1998). At the time and given the difficulties that could have been encountered because of the *de facto* division of the island, all efforts were focused solely on achieving the national goal of EU accession and any thoughts on creating a permanent institutional structure that would focus on coordination of EU affairs following EU entry were premature.

Despite some initial obstacles caused by the then Minister of Finance Christodoulos Christodoulou, who felt threatened by the presence of the Chief Negotiator, Vassiliou enjoyed the necessary political backing by President Clerides that allowed him to progress with the accession negotiations timely and efficiently. The remarkable performance of the RoC was noted in the Commission Reports and Cyprus became the first country to successfully conclude its accession negotiations within the agreed timeframe. Cyprus was officially given the green light to become a full EU Member State at the Copenhagen European Council (December 2002) and, importantly, even though the 'Cyprus problem' was still unresolved, it was decided that the entire island would be joining the EU. This was considered a diplomatic triumph for the Governments of Cyprus and Greece.

Soon after, in February 2003, presidential elections were held in Cyprus and Tassos Papadopoulos replaced Glafcos Clerides as President of the Republic. Shortly after taking over, President Papadopoulos appointed Takis Hadjidemetriou to replace George Vassiliou as Chief Negotiator for the Accession of Cyprus to the EU (CoM Decision 57.627, 3 April 2003). On 16 April 2003, the President of the RoC signed the Treaty of Accession of Cyprus to the EU and he acknowledged the exemplary way in which accession negotiations had been carried out.

With the conclusion of negotiations, President Papadopoulos had to decide if and how the position of the Chief Negotiator for the Accession of Cyprus to the EU would evolve. It is believed that President Papadopoulos acknowledged the beneficial impact of having a coordination mechanism and the need to give it a permanent structure so as to enhance Cyprus' participation in the EU and the country's harmonization with EU requirements. As a result, in June 2003, shortly after the Accession Treaty was ratified, the Government decided to change the title of the 'Chief Negotiator' to 'Coordinator for Harmonisation of the Republic of Cyprus with the EU' (CoM Decision 58.101, 18 June 2003).

During this period, Cyprus was going through a process of intense negotiations regarding the 'Cyprus problem' that resulted in a proposed UN peace settlement on which the people of Cyprus were asked to vote just days before the official accession to the EU. The proposed settlement (also known as the 'Annan Plan') polarized and divided society; amidst a highly confrontational environment, the Coordinator for Harmonisation of the Republic of Cyprus with the EU, Mr. Hadjidemetriou, resigned from his post, citing differences with the Government over the proposed peace settlement. Filling the post was not the first priority of the President at the time, as he had to handle the repercussions from the referendum result.

While the dust had yet to settle from the referendum outcome, MFA officials allegedly pushed to postpone the appointment of a replacement for Hadjidemetriou. Their primary aim was to ensure that the creation of such a mechanism would be within the MFA and their Ministry's authority would not be jeopardized. As a result, two years after the resignation of Hadjidemetriou, the post of Coordinator for Harmonisation of the RoC remained empty and essentially became defunct. This development marked the first missed opportunity for the Government to take advantage of the critical juncture of EU entry and introduce a permanent institution, sidelining any concerns that this could possibly challenge the *status quo* and the prevailing balance of power among Government services and ministries.

President Papadopoulos, however, seemed determined to establish a permanent coordination mechanism and asked the MF and the MFA to make suggestions on the formation of a service that would centrally administer and coordinate EU-related issues. The two ministries failed to agree on a common proposal and on 26 April 2006 the President suggested that an EU Office under the President of the Republic should be created (CoM Decision 63.696, 26 April 2006). The President intended that this service would: 1) allow Cyprus to efficiently form a national position on horizontal issues; 2) enable the country to form the necessary alliances on all issues; 3) aid in the uploading of Cypriot policy preferences where possible; and 4) secure the efficient downloading of EU law at the national level. The relevant CoM's decision highlighted that in no way did the proposed service intend to undermine the role of the ministries, which remained responsible for defining and forming their positions. By reaffirming the role of the ministries, the Government aimed to address possible concerns and objections over potential loss of authority.

Just weeks after the Government's decision and as part of a reshuffle, the Minister of Foreign Affairs was replaced with Giorgos Lillikas, who took over on 13 June 2006. With the appointment of a new Minister, there was a renewed effort by the MFA to overturn the Government's decision for an EU Office under the President and delay its implementation indefinitely. It effectively succeeded in doing so and the decision taken in April 2006 was never implemented during Papadopoulos's term in office, which ended in February 2008.

3.2 The second critical juncture: the EU Council Presidency

The presidential elections in February 2008 brought a change in Government, with Demetris Christofias, leader of the left-wing AKEL Party (*Ανορθωτικό Κόμμα Εργαζομένου Λαού* – Progressive Party of the Working People), replacing Tassos Papadopoulos. With the Herculean task of the EU Council Presidency in mind, the newly elected Government decided in August 2008 on the formation of a 'team' (*Επιτελείο*) that would be placed directly under the President and would act as the central point for preparing the Republic at an organizational and administrative level for the EU Presidency (CoM Decision 67.611, 27 August 2008). The decision of the Government did not provide a clear institutional and legal status to this proposed formation.

Furthermore, and in addition to the team set up for the EU Presidency, on 14 April 2009 the CoM reviewed the issue of a permanent coordination mechanism. With reference to the non-implementation of the 26 April 2006 decision, the Government acknowledged that the lack of a coordination service for European affairs had practical negative repercussions for the country. These had to do with the inability to absorb EU funds, the disregarding of Cyprus' official positions on various issues at EU level, and the inability to form coalitions for the promotion of the country's interests. As a result, it was decided to create a coordination service for European issues. During the same CoM meeting, it was decided that Andreas Moleskis (a high-ranking civil servant from the Planning Bureau) would be appointed as head of the team for the EU Presidency.

Even though the Government had decided upon a permanent coordination service for EU affairs, it would once again prove impossible to bring the plan to fruition. Government officials considered that, because of the revived negotiations between the two communities over the 'Cyprus problem', it would be best to delay the establishment of this new government institution, which could possibly lead to constitutional complications. At the same time, the Government decided to place extra emphasis on the challenges associated with the EU Presidency and to support the *ad hoc* team created under Andreas Moleskis. This scenario suited Moleskis, who planned that this team would end up taking over as the coordination service after the end of the EU Presidency.

Nonetheless, mid-way through its term in office, the Government faced other unforeseen economic and political challenges in addition to the scheduled EU Council Presidency. First of all, it became clear that the international financial crisis would after all have significant adverse effects on the otherwise robust Cypriot economy. The Government was accused of reacting sluggishly to international financial developments and to the successive downgrades of the Cypriot economy by international credit rating agencies, initiated by Standard & Poor's downgrading in November 2010. Furthermore, the President's engagement in the negotiation process with the T/C community sparked a reaction from the so-called 'hard-line' parties that participated in the Government coalition; President Christofias was attacked for making 'generous concessions' at the negotiating table (Papadopoulos 2011).

The Government tried to juggle with the political and economic challenges but the situation almost spiralled out of control on 11 July 2011 when a massive blast of confiscated arms at the country's naval base not only caused the death of thirteen men but also left the main power station on the island in pieces, pushing the Cypriot economy further down the road to recession. Amidst unparalleled social and political unrest and an unprecedented media attack, the last remaining coalition partner withdrew from the Government in

August 2011, leaving President Christofias and his party AKEL in political isolation.

In such a hostile environment, the work of the Government was rendered even more difficult, and reaching a political consensus on any decision was close to impossible. Acknowledging this new reality, the Government did not even consider the possibility of implementing its pending decision to set up a permanent institution for the coordination of EU affairs.

Furthermore, Andreas Moleskis came under the media's spotlight in relation to his questionable hiring practices and was forced to resign from his post on 22 June 2011, thus adding further to the Government's woes. In deciding on his replacement and in an attempt to avoid political friction, the Government opted for a non-political appointment. Ambassador Mavroyiannis, with previous experience as Head of Cyprus' Permanent Representation in Brussels, was offered the position, though he set specific prerequisites before accepting the post, the most important of these being that the existing service would be given the necessary legal standing.

On 3 October 2011, Parliament passed the relevant legislation that provided for the appointment of a European Affairs Deputy Minister to head the Secretariat for the EU Presidency, with an expiry date just after the completion of the EU Presidency (law 123(I)/2011). The appointment of a Deputy Minister was presumably in violation of the constitution, however, the temporary nature of the appointment dispensed with any such legal concerns. Furthermore, for the first time the term 'Secretariat' (as opposed to the term 'team') was mentioned in an official document for the institution under the Deputy Minister of European Affairs, which was staffed mostly by Planning Bureau personnel and would take over the administrative and political coordination of the Presidency.

This arrangement proved successful for the Government and allowed for the smooth, productive, and successful cooperation of all involved Government services. The success of the Cyprus Presidency was even acknowledged at the European level through public statements by EU officials (EurActiv 2012).

The non-permanent nature of the Secretariat meant that the authority of the MFA or any other ministry was not threatened in any way. Ambassador Mavroyiannis was not seen as a threat by the MFA's high-ranking career civil servants but more as a competent diplomat (colleague) with whom they could cooperate; conversely, Moleskis was considered to have a secret agenda and long-term political aspirations to head a permanent EU affairs coordination mechanism independent from the MFA. In addition, the precisely defined EU Presidency mandate of the European Affairs Deputy Minister clearly confined his authority and did not allow him any role and/or involvement in any other policy-related issues.

Having a political appointee to head the Secretariat of the EU Presidency resembled the role former President Vassiliou had enjoyed in successfully coordinating/leading accession negotiations. What is more, once again the temporary nature of a coordination arrangement confirmed that Cyprus, while facing a second critical juncture (the EU Presidency), could not overcome rigid inter-institutional obstacles in order to implement what was considered a much needed decision to create a permanent coordination mechanism.

4 An economy in distress – dealing with the financial crisis

The international financial crisis soon revealed the precarious position of the disproportionately large banking sector in Cyprus and other structural weaknesses in the economy (Pegasiou 2013). The economy was soon caught in a downward spiral, which was reflected in a series of downgrades by international credit rating agencies that came to a head in May 2011, when government bonds were rated as 'junk', essentially cutting the Government off from international financial markets.

The option of involving the EU and the IMF, as other Eurozone countries had already done, was an ideological anathema to the left-wing State in office, which could not light-heartedly agree to the associated neo-liberal doctrine. It thus pursued alternative options and managed to secure a bilateral 2.5 billion Euro loan from Russia in November 2011. This settlement could have potentially allowed the Cypriot Government the time to take the necessary measures that could reinstate the country's lost credibility in the financial markets and thus avoid a financial loan from the EU and the IMF. In hindsight, the bilateral loan simply postponed the inevitable and less than a year later Cyprus was left with no other option than to resort to the EU and the IMF for emergency financial assistance. Cyprus' official request on 25 June 2012 came barely a week before the country took over the EU Presidency and less than eight months before presidential elections.

Importantly, at the time of the request, Cyprus had no established mechanism for EU-related affairs that could have potentially taken over the coordination of the negotiations and later on overseen the implementation of the MoU. The European Affairs Deputy Minister's mandate clearly included no provision for him to assume any sort of role in any policy area apart from the EU Presidency and his involvement in the negotiations with the Troika was out of the question.

It was assumed that the MF, being *de facto* the most relevant institution, would take a leading role concerning negotiations with the Troika, however President Christofias also pursued an active role by engaging directly in negotiations. A proudly self-proclaimed communist, President Christofias publicly repeated that his Government would not easily succumb to pressures for stinging austerity and other neo-liberal policies (Smith 2012). The Government seemed eager to stage a fight with the 'ruthless' lenders and was less concerned about a possible delay in the agreement than its primary aim which was to reach a deal that did not pose a threat to social cohesion.

In order to ensure that the Government's position was effectively promoted, the President set up an *ad hoc* interministerial committee that would negotiate with the Troika. This committee consisted of those ministers considered to be the President's most trusted political associates and the Minister of Finance, although evidently the latter, a former banker, was rather an outsider, as he did not share the same political background.

Acknowledging that the MF technocrats were closer to the position of the Troika than of the Government, the President sought an active role for the interministerial committee in the negotiations. At the same time, he personally met frequently with Troika representatives to ensure that the Government's position was correctly presented. The Minister of Finance evidently did not have the full backing of the President and was caught between a rock and a hard place, a setting that did not allow him to act in a timely manner (Phileleftheros 2012). In many cases in which there were issues of dispute between the Government and Troika officials, negotiations were transferred to the Presidential Palace, where the President eagerly participated, but did not always have a positive record of achieving middle-ground consensual solutions.

The inability of the Government in office and the Troika officials to see eye to eye was essentially the result of the clash of ideologies. Any agreement by a left-wing Government to the Troika's proposed measures would certainly carry an unbearable political cost. As a result, negotiations for the Cypriot rescue package were protracted and lasted far longer than the negotiations with any of the previous countries who had requested aid (see Table 5.1). The opposition parties even accused the Christofias Government of deliberately dragging out negotiations and not adopting an effective national strategy in order to avoid signing a final agreement before the presidential elections in February 2013.

Table 5.1 The timeframe of MoU with the Troika

Country	**Request for Aid**	**Agreement**	**Bail-out Exit**
Greece	23 April 2010	3 May 2010	Pending
Ireland	21 November 2010	28 November 2010	December 2013
Portugal	6 April 2011	4 May 2011	June 2014
Cyprus	25 June 2012	23 March 2013	March 2016

Nevertheless, an initial staff-level agreement was finally reached in November 2012. Its conclusion, however, was contingent upon the determination of the banking sector's recapitalization needs. These were to be calculated by PIMCO, a private global investment management firm. PIMCO's report came just a few days prior to the February 2013 elections; however, by then it had become obvious that the final agreement would be concluded by the newly elected President. Nevertheless, the implementation of the draft memorandum agreement was initiated and a first set of measures was approved by Parliament in December 2012.

4.1 The signing and implementation of the Memorandum

In the February 2013 elections, presidential candidate and president of the main opposition party, the right-wing DISY (*Δημοκρατικός Συναγερμός* – Democratic Rally), Nicos Anastasiades, enjoyed a secure victory. The newly elected President took over on 1 March 2013 and in the first Eurogroup meeting following the elections it was noted that:

> With the new Government now in place in Cyprus, the Eurogroup is confident that a swift conclusion of the negotiations towards a Memorandum of Understanding can be reached. The Eurogroup welcomes the commitment of President Anastasiades, reiterated by Minister Sarris, to closely cooperate with Cyprus' European partners towards the earliest possible completion of the loan agreement.
>
> (Eurogroup 2013)

The most pressing issue on the agenda of the newly elected Government was the agreement of a financial request package with international lenders. With time running out and the available government liquidity dangerously depleting, negotiations between the newly elected Government and the international lenders did not last more than a few weeks. The long-awaited agreement concerning Cyprus' financial request was enforced following two historic Eurogroup meetings in March 2013 between which there was a ten-day bank holiday. The final agreement, offered in a 'take it or leave it' manner to the Cypriot Government, included an unprecedented bail-in of depositors for the two largest banks in Cyprus. In essence, such a provision could have potentially proven carried a lethal hit to the Cypriot financial sector, upon which the economy of the country relied greatly. While acknowledging the harsh treatment that resembled more of a 'guinea pig' experiment for future European bail-in of deposits, Government officials, having no other option that would not endanger Eurozone and EU membership, accepted the proposed programme and confirmed their commitment to implementing it as the only way out of the crisis (Kasoulides 2013).

Following the agreement, there was a change in the MF and Harris Georgiades, a close and trusted political associate of the President, was appointed as Minister with the primary aim of securing the timely implementation of the MoU. The newly appointed Minister was given the authority to lead discussions with Troika officials regarding the progress of the programme. Though the President was directly involved in the negotiations that led to the agreement, he now seemed eager to take a step back and allow his Minister to take over.

Upon taking over, Minister of Finance Georgiades identified a gap in both the coordination of Government services and the communication with the Troika, and was alarmed since this rather inefficient method of interaction could potentially harm the Government in its effort to implement the MoU. Therefore, before the first Troika review in July 2013 and in an attempt to deal with this gap, the Government decided on the *ad hoc* coordination mechanism that would take over monitoring the implementation of the MoU. The MF would clearly have the leading role in this arrangement. At the political level, the Minister of Finance would be heading the inter-ministerial committee, which also included the Minister of Commerce, Industry and Tourism, the Minister of Labour and Social Securities, the Minister of Health, and the Deputy Minister to the President. In addition, the Planning Bureau would be coordinating the interaction between the relevant government services at the technocratic level (CoM Decision 74.995, 24 April 2013).

The Minister of Finance's intention was to fully utilize all the relevant units and departments of the MF so as to create a mechanism that would enhance the communication of government services with the Troika. This proved to be more of a practical rather than an institutional arrangement, since no new institutions were formed but existing structures were better utilized instead. Minister Georgiades had no intention of relating this *ad hoc* arrangement to the creation of a permanent coordination mechanism for European affairs under the MF, because his sole purpose was to efficiently implement the MoU in the short run as a national strategy for exiting the MoU without any delay.

Within the course of the programme implementation, the task of coordination was transferred from the Planning Bureau (renamed Directorate General for European Programmes, Coordination, and Development [DGEPCD] in November 2013 – law 127(I)/2013) to the Unit of Strategic Coordination and Cooperation under the Minister of Finance. This arrangement was merely an intraministerial issue that did not involve any other ministries.

Under this revised title, the DGEPCD has a number of directorates, including a Directorate for European Funds (which is responsible for, *inter alia*, the Multiannual Financial Framework, Cohesion Policy, and European Structural and Investment Funds Programming) and a Directorate for European Programmes. The DGEPCD's authority for coordinating European-funded programmes has been confirmed, albeit with no provision for an overall coordinating role on European horizontal issues. This was something that at least in theory should still be the responsibility of the MFA.

4.2 Government–Troika relations during the implementation phase

The relationship that developed between the MF and the Troika during the implementation phase of the programme proved to be smooth and productive. From the start the two sides set common strategic objectives, such as the need to rectify budget imbalances, promote structural changes that would enhance growth potential, overhaul the civil service, and improve the soundness and resilience of the banking sector. This, of course, entailed a number of unpopular measures that were adopted by Parliament before the change in government in 2013 and were based on the interim agreement reached in November 2012. Among other things, there were public sector wage cuts, a compulsory contribution by public sector employees to their health care scheme, an increase in the retirement age, social transfer cuts (as part of a social welfare reform that introduced a guaranteed minimum income scheme and targeted benefits to those most in need), and a reduction in pension benefits. Furthermore, measures targeting the financial and banking sectors included a modern and effective foreclosure and insolvency framework that would allow for an improved handling of non-performing loans, which still remain one of the most significant challenges in the Cypriot economy since they account for almost 60 per cent of all loans.

In addition, certain institutional arrangements have been introduced since March 2013. Importantly, the Fiscal Responsibility and Budget System Law (FRBSL) (law 20 (I)/2014) was adopted in 2014, which aims to improve Cyprus' fiscal performance by setting out a broad framework of fiscal rules, discipline, and transparency. Prior to the Eurozone crisis, Cyprus had lacked a solid fiscal framework, as there were no elements of a balanced-budget rule or independent budgetary councils in the constitution (Pantazatou 2014). Now the FRBSL sets the budget process into a medium-term framework consistent with a strategic approach to planning both domestic resources and resources from the EU and other sources. The law provides for, amongst other things, the introduction of modern principles for budgeting and ensuring financial transparency on the basis of public finance management best practices. Based on this framework, line ministries will enjoy a significant role in planning and executing the budget in the policy areas for which they are responsible. They will do so by implementing new procedures when drafting their budgets, including the formulation of a Strategic Plan and a three-year budget for achieving their strategic goals. In overseeing this system, the MF has been assigned an enhanced monitoring role.

The FRBSL has also provided for the creation of a Fiscal Council independent from the MF, with a clear mission to make timely and effective public interventions, aimed at the avoidance of a fiscal derailment and the safeguarding of fiscal stability. Through its annual autumn report, the Fiscal Council seeks to assess macroeconomic and budgetary projections, compliance with the fiscal rule, and the automatic correction mechanism and review of the financial policy including financial measures.

To pass the measures in Parliament, the Government of President Anastasiades had to overcome the loss of majority support, following the February 2014 withdrawal from the Government coalition of DIKO (*Δημοκρατικό Κόμμα* – Democratic Party), which cited unbridgeable differences with the President on the 'Cyprus problem'. Despite merely having the support of one party in Parliament, the Government was fortunate to achieve majority support on a number of pieces of MoU-related legislation by cooperating with opposition parties (DIKO especially), a practice indicative of a process of 'consensual politics' that takes place on the island on various issues (Mavratsas 2003). Certain opposition parties opted for what they named a 'sensible and responsible stance' that secured economic and financial stability, though they pushed for certain modifications on the proposed MoU-related legislation. The MF tried to incorporate the proposed amendments in order to secure majority support in Parliament without losing the approval of the Troika. In doing so, it effectively acted as the mediator between Parliament and the Troika, and thus successfully overcame obstacles that could potentially have derailed the strenuous efforts to implement the MoU.

4.3 The implementation of the MoU – success or failure?

The Minister of Finance repeatedly stated that the Government of Cyprus should have adopted many of the provisions in the agreed MoU regardless of the outcome of the vote. Instead of viewing the adjustment programme as an externally imposed anathema, the Minister of Finance chose to demonstrate political ownership and treat it as Cyprus' own programme. Even when it came to harsh economic policies, instead of opting for a blame-shift approach and accusing the 'evil Troika', the Minister highlighted the 'necessity' of taking such measures. This non-confrontational approach has been the focus of criticism, especially by the left-wing AKEL, which opposes what they call

Table 5.2 Gross domestic product – compared to the quarter of the previous year (percentage change)

Date	2012				2013				2014				2015		
	Q1	Q2	Q3	Q4	Q1	Q2	Q3	Q4	Q1	Q2	Q3	Q4	Q1	Q2	Q3
% change	-1.4	-2.4	-2.2	-3.9	-5.8	-6.6	-5.5	-5.9	-4.0	-2.1	-2.1	-1.8	+0.2	+1.2	+2.3

Source: Ministry of Finance – Statistical Service (2016)[5].

'neo-liberal, austere, and anti-social' policies and the Government's keen alignment to them (Simerini 2014).

Nearly three years after the commencement of the adjustment programme, in January 2016, the Minister of Finance, while speaking before the European Parliament's Economic and Monetary Affairs Committee in Brussels, announced that Cyprus would be able to complete the IMF/ESM (European Stability Mechanism) programme on time (i.e. by March 2016); he defined it as a story of economic recovery, optimism, and hope. It has been argued that economic recovery could have come even faster if confidence in the banking sector and the economy in general had not been lost due to the unprecedented bail-in imposed on depositors (Charalambous 2015).

More than three years after being elected, the Anastasiades Government claimed, in contrast to the arguments of the previous AKEL Government, that successful fiscal adjustment and structural reform did not necessarily deepen the recession. The economy has already experienced positive growth rates (see Table 5.2) while the financial sector has stabilized to a large extent. Nevertheless, the opposition parties continue to criticize the increasing equality divide and the unemployment figures (unemployment has remained at historically unprecedented high levels, exceeding 15 per cent for the past five years).

At the international level, the country's lenders have viewed the Government's overall cooperative and coherent stance in a positive manner and have praised it in the numerous assessment reports issued. Nevertheless, they always stress the remaining underlying obstacles that need to be dealt with. However, in June 2015, Mark Lewis (IMF Mission Chief for Cyprus) commented, in an interview with *IMF Survey*, that:

> Performance under the programme has been good over the past year. Public finances have exceeded expectations, structural reforms have proceeded, and the authorities' ownership of the programme has remained high. Still though, important challenges remain for the programme and beyond ... Three priorities stand out. Firstly, banks should be in a position

to extend new credit to the economy. Secondly, the corporate sector should attract more foreign direct investment. And thirdly, the Government should continue to steer down public debt, which remains very high.

Cyprus has also, on many occasions, been considered a 'success story' as the country successfully exited the MoU programme within the agreed three-year timeframe (Stockwatch 2016). The depicted story of success is nevertheless something the opposition parties strongly dispute.

5 The last failed attempt for an EU affairs coordination mechanism

Simultaneously with the *ad hoc* coordination arrangement set for the effective implementation of the MoU, the Government attempted to tackle the long-standing issue concerning the creation of a permanent coordination structure for EU affairs.

Given the success of the Secretariat established for the EU Council Presidency, which was dissolved in January 2013, the aim of the MFA was to push for a permanent coordination mechanism for EU affairs; in contrast to the Secretariat, this mechanism would be under the MFA's control. This arrangement would focus on the coordination of EU affairs specifically, while there was no intention of assuming any authority over the implementation of the financial adjustment programme, which was (generally) accepted to be under the responsibility of the MF.

In the proposal submitted and approved by the Council of Ministers (CoM Decision 76.198, 19 December 2013), the European Union Division within the MFA was given the task of ensuring that the necessary coordination of EU affairs between government services takes place. This new arrangement effectively provides for coordination at three levels, yet there is no provision for a political appointment (i.e. the appointment of a Deputy Minister of European Affairs) that would head the coordination mechanism. Specifically, at the top level, the mechanism involves a ministerial committee for EU affairs chaired by the Minister of Foreign Affairs. At the second level, the Coordinating Committee involves the permanent secretaries of the ministries headed by the Deputy Minister under the President. Finally, the coordination at the third level takes place between the officials from the EU divisions of the ministries, with the relevant EU division of the MFA having the leading role. Notably, the EU division of the MFA also acts as the secretariat at all levels for this coordination mechanism.

More than two years after the Government's decision to create such a coordination mechanism, it is widely acknowledged that this arrangement has proven dysfunctional and has failed to bring about the desired results. This is primarily a result of the decision not to provide for a political appointment to head this mechanism, something that essentially deprived the mechanism of the necessary political clout that would allow it to exercise authority and perform its duties. Though President Anastasiades had, prior to his election, committed to address legal restrictions and appoint a number of deputy ministers (including one for European Affairs), this option has not been pursued and no efforts have been made to attain the necessary legal authorization to do so.

In addition, the other ministries have acted with a 'turf mentality' and, not being comfortable with the leading role assigned to the MFA, have refused to genuinely cooperate. They consider that deciding upon a more cooperative stance would constitute conceding ground in an ongoing implicit interministerial rivalry. In addition, another issue of more practical importance is the lack of personnel within the ministries. Having more personnel would allow each ministry to assign to a civil servant the exclusive responsibility for liaising with the coordination mechanism.

As a result, the initiative of the Government to set up a coordination mechanism has failed to deliver the desired results. Committees at both the ministerial and permanent-secretary level in the coordination mechanism have hardly ever met, while meetings between the EU divisions of the ministries have been problematical. Deeply embedded practices and attitudes within the ministries that can be traced historically have in practice acted as a barrier to the Government's decision; the Government itself has shown a lukewarm and rather indifferent reaction to the resulting failure of its decision.

Consequently, *ad hoc* coordination arrangements are adopted in those cases where two or more ministries may have different approaches towards important horizontal issues. It is often the case that for important issues prior to European Council meetings, the Government spokesman Nicos Christodoulides (a competent diplomat who also acts as Sherpa officer at the European level, i.e. the European affairs advisor to the President) takes over a mediating role and intervenes in order to bridge any communication breakdown between the ministries involved.

Overall, Cyprus' inconsistent and ineffective approach to the coordination of EU affairs is in accordance with Kassim's categorization of Cyprus' EU policy coordination characterized by relatively limited ambition and a lack of centralized structure. The reliance of successive governments on *ad hoc* arrangements only when deemed absolutely necessary and the failed attempts to establish a permanent structure reflect Cyprus' inability to have a continuous involvement on all policy fronts that are open at the European level. The country has been preoccupied with the downloading of EU requirements without seeking to become an active player at the European level. In particular, the lack of a permanent structure has allowed for a system with numerous players that operate in a non-hierarchical manner.

Two other institutions (the Permanent Representation in Brussels and Parliament) that could potentially take a more active role have not been assigned such power. On the one hand, the Permanent Representation in Brussels acts like a facilitator/mediator rather than an influential actor. It has always been headed by a career diplomat (although in theory the President has the power to appoint individuals outside the MFA) who acts according to the direction and the specific framework prescribed by the MFA, but he/she is not assigned any authority to pursue policy coordination. Also, given the presidential system in Cyprus and the clear distinction between the executive and the legislative branch, Parliament has not been involved in the coordination of EU affairs at the ministerial level. Its involvement became more direct and influential during the period of implementation of the MoU when politically costly and unpopular measures had to be adopted.

6 Conclusion

The case of Cyprus stands out as an example of numerous failed attempts to create a permanent coordination mechanism for EU affairs. While it has been argued that a rational approach is helpful in explaining the creation of *ad hoc* temporary institutional arrangements that were essential for accomplishing significant milestones in Cyprus' pursuit of EU related requirements, it is necessary to apply a sociological and historical perspective to understand its inability to form a permanent institutional structure. Undoubtedly, legal obstacles stemming from its incapacity to directly revise the constitution (e.g. with a provision for additional ministers) have been an important factor, but, in addition, the strength and authority accumulated and the culture nurtured in a path-dependent process by the rigidly structured civil service have proven an insurmountable obstacle.

Despite the power enjoyed by Cypriot Presidents and the acknowledgement on their part of the need for such a mechanism, this structure has never materialized. The last failed attempt merely confirms that institutional rigidity and entrenched attitudes do not allow for a redefinition of the balance of power and authority between the ministries.

With reference to the MoU, the MF was rightly considered the most relevant institution to take over the responsibility of overseeing its implementation and leading the communication with the Troika. By making use of the existing institutional structure within the MF, the Minister of Finance has secured a successful coordination of the relevant government services and the execution of the majority of the relevant requirements stemming from the MoU. In doing so, the MF did not set out to extend its authority and take over a broader coordinating role on European affairs via, for example, the reformed DGEPCD. This possibility was never considered, although the MFA's performance in this respect had been disappointing.

Nonetheless, it is worth noting that during the financial crisis the role of the MF has undoubtedly been advanced as it became the key point of interaction with the international lenders and the focal point for the required reforms at the national level. Furthermore, the MF has been assigned an enhanced coordinating and supervisory role in the formation and implementation of future government budgets, stemming from the FRBSL. At the same time, the Minister of Foreign Affairs did not attempt to intervene in any way in the work of the MF, either directly or indirectly (via, for example, the Permanent Representation in Brussels).

Consequently, given that at both the European and the national level financial and economic affairs have become the dominating issues on the agenda, the MFA in some way comes out as the institution that, compared to the MF, has lost influence in the prevailing domestic power equilibrium, although this has not been reflected in any formal institutional adjustments by the Government.

Notes

1 It is crucial to note that the Government of the RoC has been run exclusively by G/Cs since 1963. In 1964, the Supreme Court ruled that the functioning of the Government must continue on the basis of the 'Doctrine of Necessity'. Following this development the Government has continued to enjoy international recognition and legitimacy.

2 For the application of the 'Doctrine of Necessity', the following prerequisites must be satisfied: 1) an imperative and inevitable necessity or exceptional circumstances should exist; 2) there should be no other remedy available; 3) the measure taken should be proportionate to the necessity; and, finally, 4) the measure must be of a temporary character limited to the duration of the exceptional circumstances.

3 The Diplomatic Office and, more recently, the Negotiator's Office (established in 2013 and again staffed by career diplomats) have had the primary responsibility for preparing documents, drafting proposals, and the strategy of the G/C community in the intercommunal talks.

4 The Planning Bureau was established in 1961 as a separate unit under the authority of the MF. Its primary aim was to formulate the long-term development policy of the Government and at the same time oversee its implementation. It also assumed a primary role in dealing with European affairs and, for instance, was instrumental regarding the signing of the Agreement of Customs Union between Cyprus and the EEC.

5 See the website of the MF: http://www.mof.gov.cy/mof/cystat/statistics.nsf/economy_finance_11main_en/economy_finance_11main_en?OpenForm&sub=1&sel=2.

Bibliography

Capoccia G. and Kelemen R.D. (2007) 'The Study of Critical Junctures: Theory, Narrative, and Counterfactuals in Historical Institutionalism', *World Politics* 59 (3) (341–369).

Charalambous A. (2015) 'The Cyprus Adjustment Programme – Necessity or Wrong Medicine?', *Cyprus Economic Policy Review* 9 (2) (21–34).

Checkel J.T. (1999) 'Social Construction and Integration', *Journal of European Public Policy* 6 (4) (545–560).

Dowding K.M. (1995), *The Civil Service*, London, Routledge.

EurActiv (2012) 'EU leaders Hail "Successful" Cyprus Presidency', 14 December 2012, http://www.euractiv.com/future-eu/leaders-eu-summit-hail-successfu-news-516692.

Eurogroup (2013) Eurogroup Statement on Cyprus 4 March 2013, http://www.consilium.europa.eu/press/press-releases/2013/03/pdf/Eurogroup-statement-on-Cyprus.

Hall P.A. and Taylor R.C. (1996) 'Political Science and the Three New Institutionalisms', *Political Studies* 44 (5) (936–957).

IMF Survey Magazine (2015) 'Cyprus Steps Toward Sustainable Growth', https://www.imf.org/external/pubs/ft/survey/so/2015/int062315a.htm.

Kasoulides I. (2013), Speech by the Minister of Foreign Affairs, Mr. Ioannis Kasoulides, at the House of Commons, London (24 April 2013), http://www.mfa.gov.cy/mfa/mfa2016.nsf/All/414D6EB5D3D0C97CC2257FAA0030DDCA?OpenDocument.

Kassim H. (2015) 'The National Coordination of EU Policy', in Magone J.M. (ed.), *Handbook of European Politics*, London, Routledge (686–707).

Ker-Lindsay J. (2006) 'Presidential Power and Authority in the Republic of Cyprus', *Mediterranean Politics* 11 (1) (21–37).

Ker-Lindsay J. (2008) 'Presidential Power and Authority', in Ker-Lindsay J. and Faustmann H. (eds.), *The Government and Politics of Cyprus*, Bern, Peter Lang (107–124).

Mavratsas C. (2003) *Εθνική ομοψυχία και πολιτική ομοφωνία* (National Unity and Political Consensus), Athens, Katarti.

Pantazatou K. (2014) 'Constitutional Change through Euro Crisis Law: Cyprus', http://eurocrisislaw.eui.eu/wp-content/uploads/2014/03/Cyprus-FIN.pdf.

Papadopoulos N. (2011) 'Γενναιόδωρων προσφορών Χριστόφια συνέχεια…', (Christofias's Generous Concessions Continue) (Statement by DIKO Vice President Nicolas Papadopoulos on 23 September 2011), http://npapadopoulos.easyconsole.com/easyconsole.cfm/id/239.

Pegasiou A. (2013) 'The Cypriot Economic Collapse: More than a Conventional South European Failure', *Mediterranean Politics*, 18 (3) (333–351).

Phileleftheros (2012) Φιλελεύθερος Without a Remedy for the Crisis – Minister of Finance Again Left Exposed by President Christofias over Measures Χωρίς συνταγή για την κρίση – Χριστόφιας: Άφησε πάλι εκτεθειμένο τον υπουργό Οικονομικών για τα μέτρα (printed edition 2 June 2012, page 1).

Richards D. and Smith M.J. (2000) 'The Public Service Ethos and the Role of the British Civil Service', *West European Politics* 23 (3) (45–66).

Simerini (2014) 'AKEL Calls on Citizens to Protest', (ΑΚΕΛ καλεί τους Πολίτες σε εκδηλώσεις διαμαρτυρίας) (printed edition 4 March 2014 page 1).

Smith H. (2012) 'Cyprus Takes Over EU Presidency Amid Doubts Whether It Can Navigate Crisis', *Guardian*, 4 July 2012, https://www.theguardian.com/world/2012/jul/04/cyprus-eu-presidency-europe-crisis?newsfeed=true.

Stockwatch (2016) 'Cyprus Economy a Success Story', 14 January 2016, http://www.stockwatch.com.cy/nqcontent.cfm?a_name=news_view&ann_id=244893&lang=en.

Supreme Court of Justice (1985) Reference of the Supreme Court of Justice (Reference 10/85), http://www.cylaw.org/clr/1985/1985_3_2801.pdf.

6 EU coordination in Italy

(Predominantly) internally driven changes in times of crisis

Sabrina Ragone

1 Introduction

Italy's political landscape has been largely influenced by the parliamentary system adopted through the republican constitution that entered into force in 1948. It has traditionally been governed by short-lasting executives, with only a few exceptions. In fact, within the sixty-eight years since the adoption of the constitution, there have been more than sixty governments. To tackle the issue of instability, the initial proportional electoral system underwent two reforms: in 1993, a mixed system was introduced that allotted 75 per cent of parliamentary seats according to a majority vote and 25 per cent according to a proportional vote; and 2005 saw the introduction of a proportional system with the so-called 'majority prize', i.e. a mechanism that ensures the most-voted coalition receives the majority of seats. The electoral law passed in 2015 was also proportional with a 'majority prize', but it added a second ballot between the two most voted lists if no list had achieved 40 per cent in the first vote. A new electoral law is currently under parliamentary consideration after the Italian Constitutional Court declared on 25 January 2017 that some features (in particular, the second ballot) of this system were unconstitutional.

In spite of these modifications, the situation has not changed significantly, not even during the so-called 'Second Republic'. This journalistic expression identifies a political phase that started in 1993, continues today, and stems from both the new electoral law and the bipolarization of political parties, with a basic contraposition between a centre-left and a centre-right coalition. Even after this major change in Italian politics, there have been twelve governments with an average duration of approximately one year – the parliamentary term being five. Recently, scholars have pointed out that there is a need for instruments to stabilize the executive, highlighting, in particular, the fragmentation of the political spectrum (Pasquino 2015, 300 ff.).

Since the outbreak of the financial crisis in 2008, there have been five governments. Their longevity has depended, to a great extent, on the economic situation and the need to fulfil European and international expectations.

There were two administrations during the sixteenth parliamentary term (2008–2013). The Government led by Silvio Berlusconi (May 2008–November 2011) had to face the first effects of the financial crisis, such as the reduction of the gross domestic product (GDP) and, above all, the sovereign-debt crisis with the peaking of interest rates on State bonds. Indeed, the growing stock of public debt and the dwindling credibility of the Italian Government and political system led international investors to question the solidity of the Italian budget and to levy incredibly high interest rates consistent with the alleged risk. The political and media debates focused on the so-called 'spread', the yield difference between Italian and German bonds. In summer 2011, when the financial situation became unsustainable and the spread reached 400 points (in January it amounted to approximately 170), Greece, Ireland, and Portugal had already requested assistance from the International Monetary Fund (IMF) and the European Union (EU). The Italian banking sector was under pressure due to the economic crisis and the fact that national banks held a huge amount of public bonds, whose rating was lowered by the rating agency Standard & Poor's with dramatic consequences.

Furthermore, in August, J.C. Trichet and M. Draghi, former and new President of the European Central Bank (ECB), sent a 'confidential' letter[1] to the Italian Prime Minister (PM). They recommended a series of measures divided into three groups according to the target: a) measures to 'enhance potential growth'; b) measures to ensure 'the sustainability of public finances'; and c) measures to rehabilitate the public sector. The list of measures was very detailed and specific; it even indicated the kind of legislation to be passed and a series of deadlines. Soon afterwards the ECB took a paramount role in combating the crisis, even by unconventional means such as buying Member States' bonds in the secondary market in order to tackle the speculation against the Euro.

The progressive loss of trust in Italian politics from the international perspective, combined with the internal pressure, led to Berlusconi's resignation at the end of the year and to the formation of a new Government of technocrats led by Mario Monti (November 2011–April 2013). Monti had previously been appointed a lifetime senator by the President of the Republic, who also chose him to form a 'unity cabinet' for the implementation of austerity measures and structural reforms needed to tackle the sovereign debt crisis.

During the current parliamentary term, there have been three governments. The first, led by Enrico Letta (April 2013–February 2014), was also a 'President's cabinet', i.e. an executive characterized by a strong confidence relationship with the President of the Republic, similar to the Monti

Government. In its policies, this Government pursued the same targets as the previous Government. The electoral results did not provide for a consistent majority between the Chamber of Deputies and the Senate: the centre-left coalition, and in particular the Democratic Party, who had the majority in the former but not in the latter, could not govern without the support of other parties. The second Government (February 2014–December 2016) was led by Matteo Renzi, who had become the secretary of the Democratic Party at the end of 2013. His party withdrew its trust from Letta in favour of Renzi, who was then in charge of the executive for almost three years. His administration engaged in a strong reformative mission reflected in the numerous reforms passed, concerning the electoral system, the public administration, the educational system, the labour market, and, moreover, the constitutional amendment approved by Parliament and rejected in the referendum held in December 2016. Regarding the coordination of EU policies, this Government brought about several novelties both in practice and in legal terms. The new comprehensive law concerning the Italian participation in the EU had been passed in December 2012 but was implemented mainly during 2015 and 2016. The resignation of Renzi followed the result of the referendum. The President of the Republic appointed a new Government led by Paolo Gentiloni (in December 2016), who held the post of Minister of Foreign Affairs in the Renzi Government.

2 The coordination of EU policies as a relevant research question for Italy in the current political and historical context

Italy is one of the founding members of the European Communities (ECs) and is generally considered Europe-friendly. Due to its long membership, it is possible to follow the progressive adaptation of the coordination mechanisms since the early years of integration until the European Union (EU) era, thus taking into account the course of a fairly extensive time span. In fact, the European membership is considered to create constant needs for coordination for its Member States (see the comprehensive reconstructions by Kassim, Peters, and Wright 2000; Olsen 1997; and Mény, Muller and Quermonne 1996). The timeframe is very relevant in light of the diachronic comparative approach of this book, which aims to focus on the evolution of domestic systems in order to highlight patterns of convergence and divergence between the case studies and within each of them.

Furthermore, Italy presents a higher degree of complexity compared to other case studies because it is a decentralized regional State: the need for coordination not only arises among different branches of the central administration but also on different territorial levels.

Over the decades, the coordination structures have undergone several changes, in particular because of the multiplication of the actors involved both in the adoption and in the implementation of EU acts (on the evolutionary path followed during the first decades, see Ronzitti 1987, 207 ff.; Franchini 1990, 37 ff., and the *Indagine conoscitiva sulla partecipazione dell'Italia alle fasi formativa ed applicativa del diritto comunitario* [Survey on the Italian participation in the law-making and implementation of EU law] completed by the Senate in 1991). These changes have affected both the internal organization of Government (Saltari 2013; Ragone 2013; Baroncelli 2008) – in particular, the Office of the PM – and the interaction with other institutions (della Cananea 2000 and Saltari 2013). In fact, although the executive has always been and still is the main character on the stage (Kassim 2005), both Parliament and Regions have progressively acquired new powers. These changes were consistent not only with the increasing involvement of new actors in the ECs but also with the evolution of the domestic form of government, as this chapter explains later on (and as has already been highlighted by Ragone 2014, 233). Therefore, the coordination of EU policies in the Italian context must be addressed by taking into account principally the core executive, but also the other administrations involved (Franchini 1991, 775 ff.).

The approach of this chapter is coherent with the twofold nature of the research question addressed in this volume, which is both theoretical and empirical.[2] The chapter elaborates on the regulation of the coordination of EU policies but also considers the 'law in action' with a more political and practice-oriented approach. The content in this regard is based on a series of interviews carried out in 2015 and 2016 with officials working in all the coordination structures of the Italian executive. In addition to the legal and administrative facets of the coordination mechanisms, political practices are also relevant. As a consequence, an interdisciplinary perspective that combines the doctrinal reconstruction of the legal framework with the analysis of the practice is required.[3] In particular, the study investigates the changes that have occurred since the outbreak of the financial crisis in order to understand which of them are a result of the crisis and which are more likely linked to internal dynamics.

The chapter's perspective is domestic. It focuses on the Italian mechanisms in both the ascending (the formation of the national position to be defended in Brussels – uploading) and in the descending (the implementation – downloading) phase, thereby only partially considering the relationship with the Permanent Representation in Brussels.

EU membership has strengthened the executives because they participate directly in the decision-making process at the European level, as political scientists have demonstrated. This is still true today; however, the margin of manoeuvre of each Government is not that wide with regard to all those matters on which decisions are taken by majority vote and not unanimously, which obliges the Governments to negotiate (Lanchester 2009, XVIII). Nevertheless, in Italy the empowerment of the executive has not affected all ministries equally (see in this respect Goetz 2000, 211 ff.). This imbalance can be attributed to the fact that not all areas of European policy-making have such a high profile as the economic and financial facet of the European process of integration (Goetz and Meyer-Sahling 2008, 14). In this respect, the chapter investigates which branches of the Italian Government have actually assumed a relevant role in the coordination of EU policies and whether their importance depends on the contextual factors of crisis or on domestic reasons.

To do so, the study deals with the impact that European integration has had on the structure of the Italian executive and its functioning. Institutional and administrative coordination of EU policies has varied over the years and even very recently. Scholarship has identified two stages: a) the first one (until the 1980s) was characterized by centralization and primacy of the national Government with an emphasis on the Ministry of Foreign Affairs (MFA); b) the second one (until the early 2000s) was marked by the establishment of the Department for Coordination of Community Policies and the involvement of other administrations (della Cananea 2000, 107 ff.). I believe that the coordination mechanism entered into its third phase with the reforms of 2005 and 2012 analysed below.

Within this context, the question is whether and in what way the Eurozone crisis represented a critical juncture that transformed the domestic coordination system of EU policies. The chapter explains which new structures of coordination have been created and which existing structures have been improved during the last five to seven years. It examines which members of the core executive, in particular the PM, the Minister of Economy and Finance, and the Minister of Foreign Affairs, have assumed special importance as a consequence. From this perspective, the research assesses whether the coordination process has become more centralized and whether this change has depended on external pressure or endogenous political will.

Finally, according to a recent study on this topic by H. Kassim two other relevant characteristics need to be considered, namely the ambitiousness and the centralization/decentralization of EU coordination in each Member State. The first variable investigates whether Governments have a comprehensive approach (that is, they engage in negotiations on all acts independently of the specific policy) or a selective one (they choose the most important policies). According to Kassim, Italy belongs to the first category (Kassim 2015, 695), an assumption that empirical analysis has borne out. In spite of the difficult economic situations, the country has always participated in the law-making of EU acts and has tried to influence the outcomes. As for the centralized or decentralized organization, Kassim considers Italy a decentralized mechanism characterized by several actors and many veto players. In my opinion, the recent evolution of the coordination of EU policies during the Renzi Government reverses this classification as Italy moves towards more centralization.

3 The evolution of the coordination of EU policies by the core executive

At the earliest stage, between the 1950s and 1980s, the coordination mechanism presented a series of characteristics, some of which were gradually nuanced while others disappeared. The only interlocutor of the European institutions was the State, and particularly the Government. In spite of this new mission, the Government's architecture did not undergo any structural change. In fact, during this period neither specific committees nor groups were created, and the MFA was tasked with the daily management of all EC-related affairs, with some specific exceptions (della Cananea 1992).

There was no legal instrument to provide for Parliament to participate in defining European policies. The legislature was not equipped with any tools of direct interaction with the European institutions and did not have any specific functions to scrutinize the performance of the Government in European matters. The Regions did not participate either and their exclusion was due to both the so-called European 'regional blindness' and the lack of any domestic promotion of the Regions' involvement (D'Atena 1981; Bognetti 1984; later Falcon 2001, Scarciglia 2003, and Chieffi 2003, 2004).

Since then, the powers of both Parliament and Regions have changed dramatically, as is outlined in section 4. Nonetheless, the most relevant transformation of the coordination mechanism depended on the creation of the aforementioned Department for Coordination of Community Policies in 1987.[4] This Department, now named Department for European Policies (DEP), had, until 2014, a leading Minister appointed by the PM and formally nominated by the President of the Republic; he was designated a 'Minister without portfolio'. On the contrary in the Renzi and Gentiloni Governments, the post assigned to Sandro Gozi was Secretary of State for European Affairs.

The DEP has always been situated inside the Office of the PM and has been charged with coordinating EU policies in both the ascending and the descending phases of EU law. The internal organization of each ministry has been modified throughout the decades in order to create Evaluation Units with specific competences in EU-related affairs.

More generally, the regulation of the relationship with the EU must be analysed through the prism of its evolution following the establishment of the DEP. In the 1980s and 1990s, the coordination was mainly intended as an instrument for the descending phase,[5] whereas more recently it has been reinforced also in the ascending phase thanks to the changes introduced by law 11/2005.[6] The last reform was adopted through law 234/2012,[7] which provided an organic and comprehensive regulation of the institutional and normative elements of the Italian participation in the EU, taking into account the novelties of the Lisbon Treaty. This law regulates both the ascending and the descending phase in detail and introduces terminological and substantive innovations (Costato, Rossi and Borghi 2015).

Before analysing the coordination mechanisms operating within the Office of the PM, it is useful to briefly describe the role played by the MFA and the Ministry of Economy and Finance (MEF) throughout the decades.

The MFA has maintained a relevant role due to two factors. First, the Common Foreign and Security Policy is still a non-'Europeanized' policy, i.e. it is intergovernmental policy in which the MFA is the most important player. Second, the MFA represents the institutional link with the Permanent Representation in Brussels, which has been given the task of defending the Italian position within the EU, in particular in the preparatory bodies of the Council. The Representatives are involved in the tasks of the Permanent Representatives' Committee (COREPER) and they also participate in the informal working groups of the Council of the EU and in the Political and Security Committee; furthermore, they are in charge of the relations with the two consultative bodies, namely the Committee of the Regions and the Economic and Social Committee. Formally, the Permanent Representation is an office of the MFA, but its members are usually assigned to the Permanent Representation by the different ministries, thus producing distinct expertise.

The other leading actor within the core executive has always been the MEF, in particular since the launch of the Economic and Monetary Union (EMU) in the 1990s. The accession to the third phase of the EMU has been considered one of the highest strategic successes of Italy in Europe (della Cananea 2000, 106). The economic, financial, and budgetary conditions established as convergence criteria, alongside the subsequent stability and growth pacts, have valorized the role of the MEF, which became the determinant body for the access to and the management of Eurozone membership. During the last five to seven years, the status of the MEF has been elevated in practice by the necessity to respond to markets' requirements and adopt several austerity measures to cut public spending. The priority of economic and financial issues is clearly proven by the fact that Monti decided to personally hold the post of Minister of Economy and Finance at the beginning of his mandate, keeping it for eight months.

This specific case also exemplifies the progressive concentration of management in the hands of the PM and his bureaucratic apparatus. The structure of the Office of the PM has progressively been adapted through the creation of specialized bodies in order to tackle the challenges of European integration faster and more effectively. In spite of these efforts, the delayed implementation issue has not been overcome.

3.1 The internal bodies of the Office of the PM

In contrast with other Member States' systems of coordination, the Italian model has been characterized by the existence of both a Minister of European Affairs (since 2014, Secretary of State) and a coordination structure within the Office of the PM (Ragone 2014, 229 ff.). The coordination depends on three structures within the executive: the DEP; the Interministerial EU Committee (*Comitato interministeriale per gli affari europei*, CIAE); and the Technical Evaluation Committee (*Comitato tecnico di valutazione*, CTV).

3.1.1 The Department for European Policies

The Department for European Policies (DEP) is the leading actor in all the phases of EU decision-making and implementation processes.[8] It is the supporting administrative structure for the Government and, in particular, for the PM in the activities related to the Italian participation in European law-making and subsequent execution. It is tasked with the coordination of the competent national administrations, the Regions, the private actors involved, and the society in the ascending phase in order to define the Italian position to be defended within the European institutions. This function is performed in collaboration with the MFA.

The Minister of European Affairs has been – and the Secretary of State for European Affairs now is – the PM's delegate to participate in the general-affairs configuration of the Council of the EU; to promote and coordinate the ascending phase; to promote and coordinate the implementation of EU policies (descending phase), taking care of the quality of the corresponding domestic measures and the timing of application in order to avoid violating any obligations; and to facilitate the participation of Parliament in the law-making process. Recently the DEP has had to work closely with the MEF on the economic reforms and with the MFA on the Italian Presidency of the Council of the EU (July–December 2014).[9]

During the decision-making process in the European institutions, the DEP monitors how the negotiations evolve in order to foster constant adaptation of the Italian position according to the progress of the debates. In the descending phase, the DEP offers administrative support and follows the parliamentary legislative procedure for the execution or integration of EU laws. In general, it supports the Regions and all administrations that have to implement EU sources of law. The institutions with which the DEP cooperates more frequently are: a) Parliament (e.g. to prepare the documentation and the periodic reports and to monitor the implementation of European norms); b) the State-Regions Conference (*Conferenza Stato-Regioni e Province Autonome di Trento e Bolzano*), which holds specific European sessions; and c) the other branches of government, especially the MFA and the MEF.[10] Finally, as for horizontal coordination, the DEP collaborates closely with the aforementioned Evaluation Units of the other ministries.[11]

Regarding the relationship between the DEP and the MFA and their potentially overlapping competences, the interviews revealed that the cooperation is smooth and fruitful thanks to established practices of collaboration through formal and informal channels. Additionally, the DEP works closely with the Permanent Representation in Brussels (without the filter of the MFA), recently also via video conferences.

The internal structure of the DEP has been subject to several regulations, two of which were passed after the outbreak of the financial crisis,[12] because the Office of the PM was also partially reorganized in the same period.[13] Now the DEP is divided into three offices:[14] the Office for Internal Market, Competitiveness and General Affairs; the Office for the Coordination of EU Policies; and the Office for the Coordination of State Aids.

The most relevant functions, from the perspective of this study, are performed by the Office for the Coordination of EU Policies.[15] This office is in charge of coordinating the competent administrations, the private actors, and the social operators involved in order to define the Italian position to be upheld within the EU. It constantly monitors all European decision-making processes with the aim of adapting and negotiating the domestic position; it collects the corresponding documents to inform both Parliament and Regions about the outcome of the meetings of the Council of the EU and the European Council.

The Office for the Coordination of EU Policies has a special functional and operational link with the aforementioned State-Regions Conference, which is the institutional venue of cooperation and negotiation between the activities of the State and the Regions, as well as with the State-Municipalities/Local Entities Conference; and with the MEF, with which it coordinates the activities for the national reform programme within the 'Europe 2020' strategy.

In particular, the Office for the Coordination of EU Policies is connected to the CIAE and the CTV and is divided into two services: the service for coordinating and monitoring sectoral European policies and the service for coordinating and monitoring horizontal European policies. The latter is the CIAE Secretariat.

3.1.2 The Interministerial EU Committee

The first administrative body in charge of the coordination between the different ministries in EU-related matters was the Interministerial Committee for Economic Planning (*Comitato Interministeriale per la Programmazione Economica*, CIPE), created in 1967 inside the Office of the PM.[16] At that time, it was composed of the PM and the Ministers of Foreign Affairs, of Economic Planning, of Finance, of Agriculture, and of Labour, in addition to the competent Minister for the extraordinary measures in the South and in the least developed areas of the northern Regions. Other ministers were called upon to participate in the meetings of the CIPE when matters within their competence were discussed; as were the Presidents of the Regions when regional interests were affected. Among the functions of the CIPE was the promotion of any necessary measure to harmonize the domestic economic policy with the economic policies of the other Member States of the ECs.

Over the years, the composition of the CIPE changed, but not its European focus. Its functions were transferred to the Interministerial Committee for European Communities Affairs (*Comitato Interministeriale per gli Affari Comunitari Europei*, CIACE) with law 11/2005 (Savino 2008). The role of the CIACE consisted, on the one hand, in defining the political strategies and priorities of the Government within the Italian position for the ascending phase and, on the other hand, in supervising the fulfilment of obligations under EU law.[17] Law 234/2012 named this committee CIAE (*Comitato Interministeriale per gli Affari Europei*).[18]

The CIAE is convened and chaired by the PM or the Secretary of State for European Affairs, if delegated. The Minister of Foreign Affairs, the Minister of Economy and Finance, and the Minister of Regional Affairs (a Minister without portfolio) participate in the meetings, along with others who have competences related to the acts included in the agenda. When regional or local powers are to be debated, the President of the State-Regions Conference (or a regional President when delegated) or the Presidents of the corresponding associations of local entities take part in the meetings as well.

As has been anticipated, a paramount function of the CIAE is related to the ascending phase, as it is in charge of the coordination of the positions expressed by all public and private interested actors.[19] This Committee has an extensive range of tasks, such as issuing opinions when Parliament raises a scrutiny reserve resolution and negotiating domestic policies with the Regions and the local entities.

The CIAE also has an essential role in the descending phase. It can determine the level of compliance of the internal legal system with EU law and propose urgent measures to ensure such compliance; and it can adopt guidelines for the coordination between domestic administrations concerning the enactment of the project of annual 'European law' (see section 4).

The CIAE was reformed during the financial crisis through the aforementioned law 234/2012, but its main configuration and targets remained unchanged. The debates during the passing of this law mirrored the relevance given to the mechanisms of coordination in order to achieve a better defence of national interests in the EU. The former law 11/2005 had introduced the Committee exactly for this purpose. The changes partially affected the composition (with respect to the involvement of the regional and local representatives, which is now automatic), the functioning, and the internal organization (Vella 2015, 22 ff.).[20] It is the highest political coordination structure that can count on the administrative support of the bureaucracy of the Office of the PM.

The CIAE includes a secretariat situated in the Office for the Coordination of EU Policies of the DEP. It carries out and supports formal requirements for the meetings of the CIAE by editing the minutes of the meetings of the CIAE and transmitting the conclusions to all the parties involved. The Secretariat cooperates with the CTV to research the relevant materials and acts.

Although the Committee had been regulated in 2005, it did not assume an active role during the Monti Government or during the Letta Government. In practice, the coordination was performed through the organization of informal meetings among ministers. In 2014, it was expected that the preparation for the Italian EU-Council Presidency would trigger the utilization of the Committee; however, this did not occur. Nevertheless, the current Secretary of State for European Affairs, Sandro Gozi, who was appointed in April 2014 and had been one of the promoters of bill 234/2012,[21] finally decided to make use of the CIAE.

The first meetings of the Committee were held in June 2014 with a very high-profile start. Several ministers participated in the first sessions personally, although they were later replaced by the corresponding secretaries of state. The new regulation of the CIAE's organization was passed in June 2015, and the meetings were rescheduled for every three/four weeks.

Regarding the concrete coordination of EU policies within the Office of the PM, the interviews revealed that the CIAE focuses mainly on the ascending phase. The DEP in general and the CIAE Secretariat in particular enhance the preliminary preparation for the meetings with a new organizational approach designed to achieve higher efficiency. For instance, the circulation of digital documents as well as the use of video conferences is being encouraged. The descending phase has also been greatly improved, which may be why the number of infringement proceedings against Italy has lessened since the CIAE started to operate on a constant basis.[22]

In general, the cooperation with the other administrations has proven fruitful and the CIAE Secretariat is trying to lengthen the time between the communication of the agenda and the actual meeting in order to give sufficient preparation time to smaller ministries as well. These ministries need to draw up a priority list of selected EU acts that constitute highly important issues for them; hitherto, the workload has not been distributed proportionally according to the macro- or sectorial nature of the policy. Larger ministries such as the MEF or the MFA have internal structures that enable them to deal with European issues on an ongoing basis.

In this respect, not all ministries have the capacity, or will, to profit from the CIAE in the same way; and many of them are not proactive and rely on the Office of the PM to set the agenda. This attitude stems, to a certain extent, from the lack of an established culture of coordination (Saltari 2013, 478; della Cananea 2000, 104 ff.); however, the changes introduced during the last three years seem to shift exactly in this direction. The effects of a more coordinated participation in the ascending phase are also apparent in the descending phase: the implementation of the final EU act is often much more complex in the cases in which Italy has not participated properly in the negotiations.

Finally, in terms of 'coordination of the coordination', the main issue seems to be to adjust the role of the CIAE and the CTV. The CTV also has a high-level composition and has assumed a role similar to the so-called 'pre-Council', which is a weekly preparatory meeting of all the heads of the different ministries' legislative offices held before the Council of Ministers' meeting.

3.1.3 The Technical Evaluation Committee

The functions of the current Technical Evaluation Committee (CTV) were previously assigned to the Permanent Technical Committee, which was also created by law 11/2005 within the DEP for the preparation of the meetings of the CIAE.[23] The CTV is coordinated, convened, and chaired by the director of the Secretariat of the CIAE. It is composed of general managers or specialized senior officials appointed by each minister and entitled to express the position of that specific ministry. Actually, representatives of the MFA, the MEF, as well as representatives of the Department of Cohesion and the Department for Regional Affairs (which belong to the Office of the PM)[24] always attend these meetings together with the personnel of all ministries affected by the dossiers on the agenda. Additionally, the Permanent Representative of Italy before the EU can be invited, and officials of the Upper Chamber (*Senato*) and the Lower Chamber (*Camera dei deputati*) may participate as observers. When the question at stake affects regional or local powers, representatives of each Region or of the corresponding associations of local entities also participate.

The mission of the CTV is to ensure the coordination of all actors involved in the ascending phase of the EU decision-making process and to provide preparatory assistance to the CIAE for its deliberations. In particular, the CTV gathers the opinions from the different ministries and administrations involved in the issues that are being discussed at the EU level in order to instruct and define the domestic position. To fulfil its tasks, it can collect the data and information necessary for the formation of the national position, and consult experts and relevant stakeholders. Once the decision has been taken by the CIAE, the CTV transmits it to the corresponding Italian representatives who will participate in the decision-making process at the European level. Finally, the CTV monitors the implementation of the CIAE's resolutions.

For its work, the CTV counts on the bureaucratic resources of the CIAE Secretariat.[25] This Secretariat is in charge of all support tasks necessary for the functioning of the CTV and ensures coordination with the activities of the CIAE. In general, the Secretariat takes care of the administrative requirements, such as the storage and editing of minutes and the transmission of the decisions, but also of the preparation of documents concerning the dossiers on which the CTV has to take a position.

The new regulation of the organization of the CTV was passed in July 2015, and the first meeting was held in September 2015. Since then, the CTV has met approximately every two weeks. In practice, its role is mainly consultative and organizational. However, it is not merely administrative: depending on the topic, the CTV can make quasi-final decisions (then brought to the CIAE) because the composition, as already mentioned, is very high level; the participants are usually managing directors from the ministries. Normally the position of each ministry with respect to EU acts is already manifested in the CTV; nevertheless, it can be adapted in the CIAE, which is the political venue of negotiation.

4 The changing role of Parliament and Regions

The two neglected actors during the first phase, namely Parliament and Regions, have progressively improved their position in EU affairs, particularly since the entry into force of the Lisbon Treaty (Bilancia 2012, 87 ff.; Cartabia, Lupo and Simoncini 2013).

4.1 Parliament and the EU

Both Chambers of Parliament have a standing committee devoted to European policies (the 14th Committee). The involvement of these committees in European issues has been improved by law 234/2012,[26] which expanded the range of information to be obligatorily transmitted to Parliament. The current legislation contains a very detailed regulation of the mechanisms for consultation and information of Parliament. Before the meetings of the European Council, the Government has to explain which position it intends to defend; afterwards it has to transfer the results to the corresponding parliamentary bodies. Furthermore, according to the law, the Government must keep Parliament informed on issues related to foreign and defence policy and to share the documents of the COREPER.

In addition to these general duties, there are also specific obligations concerning those policies that have particularly been affected during the financial crisis. The Italian constitution was amended in 2012 to introduce the requirement of the so-called 'balanced budget' (Articles 81, 97, 117, and 119). The new Article 81 provides that the content of the budgetary law, as well as the basic standards and criteria to ensure a balance between revenue and expenditure, and sustainability of public debt must be prescribed by a law passed by the absolute majority of the members of each chamber in compliance with the principles defined through a constitutional law. Related to this procedure, law 234/2012 establishes a specific governmental duty to inform Parliament about the coordination of the economic and budgetary policies and about the functioning of the mechanisms for financial stability (Article 4). Similarly, Article 5 devises a system to involve Parliament in the decisions related to the financial and monetary sphere, while Article 6 details how it participates in the enactment of EU normative acts.

The traditional role of the legislature in the descending phase has also been strengthened. In Italy, since the adoption of law 86/1989, the implementation of directives has been based on the so-called 'European law'. This yearly law is intended to ensure the regular adjustment of the domestic legal system in line with EU law, as well as the execution of all European obligations. Law 11/2005 maintained the general configuration and function of the 'European law', assigning the initiative to the Minister of European Affairs together with the MFA and the other ministries concerned. Since 2014, the initiative has been exercised by the PM, with the transformation of the head of the DEP into a Secretary of State.

Law 234/2012, which altered the Italian participation in EU-related affairs after the Treaty of Lisbon entered into force, brought about substantial changes. It divided the traditional 'European law' into two different acts: the 'law of European delegation' and the 'European law' (Savino 2013, 470 ff.). While the former deals with the delegation for the transposition of EU directives and all EU acts that require domestic execution, the latter contains EU law that is to be directly implemented. The Government has to present the draft of the 'law of European delegation' and, where appropriate, the 'European law' every year before the end of February. The presentation of another draft of 'law of European delegation' (pertaining to the 'second semester') is also possible before the end of July, as well as the presentation of further, more specific drafts to implement EU acts with special political, economic, and social significance. Although the prominence of the executive in the entire process – both in the initiative and in the implementation phase – is still evident, the need for co-ordination with Parliament is steadily becoming a necessary condition. In spite of this, during the years of the crisis, the legislative role of Parliament has generally decreased – its prevalent activities laying in the ratification of governmental sources of law (see Ragone 2015, 534 ff.).

4.2 Regions and the EU

Regions have gradually achieved a higher degree of involvement in the European realm, in spite of the enduring predominance of the State. On the one hand, since the mid-1990s they have been allowed to open representative offices in Brussels as a means of technical, administrative, and practical connection with the EU (at the beginning of the crisis, all Regions had an office). On the other hand, they are in charge of transposing the directives and of generally implementing those European acts that fall under their legislative competence.

Law 234/2012 has reinforced the involvement of Regions both in the law-making process and in the implementation of EU law. Under certain conditions, Regions receive relevant EU-related information and participate (or co-decide) in EU-related matters. Compared with law 11/2005, law 234/2012 introduced some innovations concerning the aforementioned State-Regions Conference, the presence of which in the CIAE has been strengthened. This Conference also holds special European sessions at least three times per year. Regional Parliaments participate in the monitoring the EU's adherance to the principle of subsidiarity. They can intervene in the ascending phase regardless of an express request by the Chambers and may adopt resolutions related to the political dialogue. Although neither the national Parliament nor the regional ones have any veto power, their involvement in EU matters is thus improving, particularly their capacity to scrutinize the corresponding executive powers (Lupo 2013).

The new regulation also refers to two other conferences: the Conference of Regions and Autonomous Provinces (which is the site of horizontal connection between the regional executives) and the Conference of the Presidents of the Regional Parliaments (which is the site of horizontal connection between the regional legislatures). The horizontal conferences are used as an informational bridge between national Government and regional institutions. These

Conferences now appoint the representatives of the Italian Regions within the EU Committee of the Regions, and they are involved, at least as observers, in different coordination mechanisms. The specific legal measures that can be adopted within the State-Regions Conference are the agreements (*intese*) and opinions (*pareri*). During the ascending phase, Regions can intervene in a twofold manner: on the one hand, they can reach an agreement with the Government on the position to be defended in Brussels concerning specific drafts that affect competences of the Regions; on the other hand, they can voice their opinions regarding the general guidelines related to the elaboration of these acts and bills when an exclusive regional competence is touched upon. As regards the descending phase, the only clear-cut powers defined by law are the Regions' opinions on the drafts of both the 'law of European delegation' and the 'European law' and their opinions on the definition of guidelines, criteria, and procedures to ensure compliance with European obligations at the regional level. Moreover, in order to provide a comprehensive coordination mechanism within the Office of the PM, the DEP can employ up to six staff members of regional administrations for its activities; these members are officially appointed by the Conference of the Regions.

Finally, the transfer of information from the Government to the Regions is strengthened and formalized, and is based mostly on the cited Conferences. This duty of information is carefully regulated in specific matters: for instance, every three months the Government has to present to Parliament and Regions – through the Conference of Regions and the Conference of the Presidents of Regions – a report on the financial flows between Italy and the EU. The attention devoted to this issue provides further proof of the increasing involvement of Parliament and the Regions in very sensitive and relevant fields.

5 Conclusion

This chapter reconstructed the evolution of the coordination system of EU policies in Italy and thereby particularly highlighted the most recent changes both in the legal framework and in practice. It clarified what influence the financial crisis and the domestic political developments have had on the coordination, explaining in parallel the shifting balance of power in the core executive and the evolving attitude towards the EU.

With respect to the influence of the external factor – i.e. the financial crisis – and the internal factor – the evolution of the political situation and leadership – the conclusion is that the domestic conditions have affected the coordination of EU policies and, generally, the way of addressing EU affairs more than the financial crisis. The predominance of the endogenous impulse to change is a constant feature of the development of the Italian executive in this field, as has already been proven regarding the reforms implemented in the 1980s and in 2005 (Ragone 2014, 233).

Since 2014 there has been a progressive centralization in many areas, which has clearly improved the protagonist role of the (Office of the) PM. In the specific field of EU policy coordination at the national level, the effects of the crisis merely supported this trend without giving a major impulse to it. The leading role of the PM in EU affairs is not novel, since it derives both from the increasing relevance of European affairs in internal politics and from the growing importance at the EU level of the European Council, where the country is represented by the PM.

The current role of the CIAE can be summarized as a threefold function: it settles the conflicts between different ministries, provides them with information, and triggers dialogue between all the administrations. Its mission is to improve coordination without adopting a hierarchical character. That the CIAE and the CTV have (finally) been made use of since 2014, thus unlocking their potential for effective coordination has mainly depended on political will. In spite of some critical elements that may be remedied in the next few years, the general opinion regarding their work is good. Finally, the reorganization of the aforementioned Conferences and the exchange of information with Parliament and Regions can be seen as a consequence of both the entry into force of the Lisbon Treaty and the domestic reforms of recent years.

As it concerns the question of whether the balance of power among the ministries has changed during the crisis, the conclusion is that there were no radical adjustments in the political equilibrium within the core executive, except for the increasingly protagonist role of the PM. The functions of the DEP have been confirmed and partially improved, with the Secretary of State undertaking to enhance the DEP's task of coordination. The MFA's role is quite stable, and the cooperation with the DEP has worked properly, albeit particularly through informal channels. The MEF has been involved in the decision-making processes due to the financial situation of the country for the most part, but it has not assumed a leading role.

Finally, interpreting the results in a broader perspective, the strengthening of the coordination system of EU policies reflects a new comprehensive approach to European affairs undertaken by the Italian Government. This approach was clarified in the programme for the Italian Presidency of the Council in 2014,[27] according to which the different facets of European integration should be analysed and tackled together as a whole, and not 'sector by sector'. Such a position is embedded in the idea of enhancing the role of Italy in the ascending phase, in order for it to be more influential in Brussels.

Notes

1 The text of the letter was, however, published in the Italian newspaper *Corriere della sera*, 29 September 2011.
2 See Chapter 1.
3 This topic has more often been the object of political science studies such as Kassim, Peters and Wright (eds.) 2000.
4 Law 183/1987, 16 April 1987, devoted to 'the coordination of the policies concerning the Italian membership of the European Communities and adjustment of the domestic legal system to European regulation'.
5 Law 86/1989, 9 March 1989, devoted to the 'general rules of the Italian participation in the European Communities law-making process and the procedures to fulfil European obligations'.
6 Law 11/2005, 4 February 2005, devoted to the 'general rules of the Italian participation in the EU law-making process and the procedures to fulfil European obligations'.
7 Law 234/2012, 24 December 2012, devoted to the 'general rules of the Italian participation in the law-making process and the implementation of EU acts and policies'.
8 See Article 18 of law 234/2012.
9 See the decree of the PM dated 23 April 2014, which contains the latest delegation in the field of European affairs.
10 For a detailed enumeration of the functions given to the DEP, see Article 2 of the organization decree of the DEP dated 25 May 2016.
11 See Article 20 of law 234/2012.
12 The two regulations are the organization decree dated 21 July 2011, which regulated the internal structure of the DEP, and the aforementioned organization decree dated 25 May 2016, which replaced the former.
13 See the decree of the PM dated 1 October 2012, regulating the general structures of the Office of the PM; last amended in 2016.
14 See Article 4-10 of the aforementioned organization decree dated 25 May 2016, in which all other offices, services, and tasks of the DEP are listed.
15 See Article 6 of the aforementioned organization decree dated 25 May 2016.
16 Law 48/1967, 27 February 1967, devoted to the 'functions and structure of the Ministry of Budget and Economic Planning and the establishment of the CIPE'.
17 This Committee was also part of the Office of the PM. The PM, the Minister of Communities' Policies, the Minister of Foreign Affairs, the Minister of Regional Affairs, and other ministers with jurisdiction in the matters included in the agenda participated in its meetings.
18 See Article 2 of law 234/2012. The previous organic regulation was included in law 11/2005.
19 For the tasks of the CIAE, see the most recent Regulation 118/2015, 26 June 2015, on the functioning of the CIAE within the Office of the PM according to Article 2 of law 234/2012.
20 The regulation can be found in Article 2 of law 234/2012.
21 He was the first signatory of bill 2888, which was presented to the Chamber of Deputies in November 2009. That initiative represented one of the bills that were finally included in law 234/2012.

22 For an overview of the decrease in infringement procedures against Italy, see the data published on the website of the DEP (www.politicheeuropee.it) concerning the number of the procedures, or the page of the European Commission devoted to Italy that shows the improvements in the evolution of the transposition deficit. (http://ec.europa.eu/internal_market/scoreboard/performance_by_member_state/italy/index_en.htm).
23 Article 19 of law 234/2012. The most recent regulation of its functions can be found in decree 119/2015, 2 July 2015, which regulates how the CTV, created within the DEP pursuant to Article 19 of law 234/2012, operates.
24 See the decree of the PM, dated 1 October 2012.
25 See Article 5 of the aforementioned decree 119/2015.
26 See Article 4-6 of the aforementioned law 234/2012.
27 See the document issued for the Presidency: *Europa. Un Nuovo Inizio. Programma per la Presidenza Italiana del Consiglio dell'Unione Europea.*

Bibliography

Baroncelli S. (2008) 'Il ruolo del Governo nell'indirizzo e il coordinamento della politica europea', in Baroncelli S. (ed.), *Il ruolo del Governo nella formazione e applicazione del diritto dell'Unione europea. Le peculiarità di un sistema costituzionale multilivello*, Turin, Giappichelli (151–179).

Bilancia P. (2012) *The Dynamics of the EU Integration and the Impact on the National Constitutional Law. The European Union after the Lisbon Treaties*, Milan, Giuffrè.

Bognetti G. (1984) 'Le regioni in Europa: alcune riflessioni sui loro problemi e sul loro destino', *Le Regioni* (6) (1087–1136).

Cartabia M., Lupo N. and Simoncini A. (eds.) (2013) *Democracy and Subsidiarity in the EU. National Parliaments, Regions and Civil Society in the Decision-making Process*, Bologna, Il Mulino.

Chieffi L. (2003) 'La nuova dimensione costituzionale del rapporto tra Regioni e Unione europea', *Democrazia e diritto* 2 (87–114).

Chieffi L. (2004) 'La nuova dimensione costituzionale del rapporto tra Regioni e Unione europea', *Democrazia e diritto* 2 (87–114).

Costato L., Rossi L. and Borghi P. (eds.) (2015) *Commentario alla legge 24.12.2012 n. 234 'Norme generali sulla partecipazione dell'Italia alla formazione e all'attuazione della normativa e delle politiche dell'Unione europea*', Naples, Editoriale Scientifica.

D'Atena A. (1981) *Le Regioni italiane e la Comunità economica europea*, Milan, Giuffrè.

della Cananea G. (1992) 'L'Italia e l'Europa: la politica «comunitaria» nel periodo iniziale del processo di integrazione (1952–1967)', in Volkmar Heyen E. (ed.), *Early European Community Administration – Jahrbuch der Europäischen Verwaltungsgeschichte*, Baden Baden, Nomos (207–222).

della Cananea G. (2000) 'Italy', in Kassim H., Peters B.G. and Wright V. (eds.), *The National Co-ordination of EU Policy. The Domestic Level*, Oxford, Oxford University Press (99–113).

Falcon G. (2001) 'La «cittadinanza europea» delle Regioni', *Le Regioni* (2) (327–343).

Franchini C. (1990) 'L'integrazione europea e il governo delle politiche comunitarie in Italia: organizzazione amministrativa e rapporto con le Comunità Europee', *Rivista di diritto europeo* 30 (1) (17–38).

Franchini C. (1991) 'L'impatto dell'integrazione comunitaria sulle relazioni al vertice dell'amministrazione. Poteri governativi e poteri amministrativi', *Rivista trimestrale di diritto pubblico* (3) (775–782).

Giuliani M. and Piattoni S. (2001) 'Italy: Both Leader And Laggard', in Zeff E.E. and Pirro E.B. (eds.), *The European Union and the Member States. Cooperation, Coordination, and Compromise*, London, Rienner (115–142).

Goetz K.H. (2000) 'European Integration And National Executives: A Cause in Search of an Effect?', *West European Politics* 23 (4) (211–231).

Goetz K.H. and Meyer-Sahling J.-H. (2008) 'The Europeanisation of National Political Systems: Parliaments and Executives', *Living Reviews in European Governance* 3 (2) (4–30).

Kassim H. (2005) 'The Europeanization of Member State Institutions', in Bulmer S. and Lequesne C. (eds.), *The Member States of the European Union*, Oxford, Oxford University Press (285–316).

Kassim H. (2015) 'The National Coordination of EU Policy', in Magone J. (ed.), *Routledge Handbook of European Politics*, London, Routledge (686–707).

Kassim H., Peters B.G. and Wright V. (2000) 'Introduction', in Kassim H., Peters B.G. and Wright V. (eds.), *The National Co-ordination of EU Policy. The Domestic Level*, Oxford, Oxford University Press (1–46).

Kassim H., Peters B.G. and Wright V. (eds.) (2000) *The National Co-ordination of EU Policy. The Domestic Level*, Oxford, Oxford University Press.

Lanchester F. (2009) 'Introduzione', in Lanchester F. (ed.), *La barra e il timone. Governo e apparati amministrativi in alcuni ordinamenti costituzionali*, Milan, Giuffrè.

Lupo N. (2013) 'National and Regional Parliaments in the EU Decision-making Process, after the Treaty of Lisbon and the Euro-crisis', *Perspectives on Federalism* 5 (2) (1–28).

Mény Y., Muller P. and Quermonne J.-L. (eds.) (1996) *Adjusting to Europe. The Impact of the European Union on National Institutions and Policies*, London, Routledge.

Olsen J.P. (1997) 'European Challenge to the Nation State', in Steunenberg B. and van Vught F. (eds.), *Political Institutions and Public Policy. Perspectives on European Decision Making*, The Hague, Kluwer Academic Publisher (157–188).

Pasquino G. (2015) 'Governments in European Politics', in Magone J. (ed.), *Routledge Handbook of European Politics*, London, Routledge (295–346).

Ragone S. (2013) 'Coordinación de las políticas europeas y transformaciones estructurales de los Ejecutivos nacionales (el caso italiano en perspectiva comparada)', *Revista General de Derecho Público Comparado*, 2013 (12) (1–13).

Ragone S. (2014) 'La coordinación gubernamental de las políticas europeas. Un análisis de derecho comparado sobre los miembros fundadores', *Estudios de Deusto* 61 (2) (213–234).

Ragone S. (2015) 'La incidencia de la crisis en la distribución interna del poder entre parlamentos y gobiernos nacionales', in Balaguer Callejón F., Azpitarte Sánchez M., Guillén López E. and Sánchez Barrilao J.F. (eds.), *The Impact of the Economic Crisis on the EU Institutions and Member States*, Cizur Menor, Thomson Reuters Aranzadi (527–550).

Ronzitti N. (1987) 'European Policy Formulation in the Italian Administrative System', *The International Spectator* (4) (207–214).

Saltari L. (2013) 'Il sistema di coordinamento', *Giornale di diritto amministrativo* (5) (475–479).

Savino M. (2008) 'L'amministrazione e l'Europa: l'eterna rincorsa', in Fiorentino L. et al., *Le amministrazioni pubbliche tra conservazione e riforme. Omaggio degli allievi a Sabino Cassese*, Milan, Giuffrè (123–167).

Savino M. (2013) 'L'attuazione della normativa europea', *Giornale di diritto amministrativo* (5) (470–474).

Scarciglia R. (ed.) (2003), *Unione Europea e autonomie regionali. Prospettive per una Costituzione europea*, Turin, Giappichelli.

Vella P. (2015) 'Articolo 2. Comitato interministeriale per gli affari europei', in Costato L., Rossi L. and Borghi P. (eds.), *Commentario alla legge 24.12.2012 n. 234 'Norme generali sulla partecipazione dell'Italia alla formazione e all'attuazione della normativa e delle politiche dell'Unione europea'*, Naples, Editoriale Scientifica (22–26).

7 Conclusion

Sabrina Ragone

1 Summing up: the objectives of the volume

The aim of this volume is to analyse the instruments set up to coordinate EU-related matters within domestic governments in times of crisis. The two *fils rouges* of the study, for the first time dealt with conjunctly in a scholarly enterprise, are the EU coordination by the executive, on the one hand, and the financial crisis, on the other hand. Consistent with this approach, the selected case studies have covered a series of EU Member States whose financial situation has been (considered) precarious during the last decade, i.e. Cyprus, Greece, Ireland, Italy, and Portugal.

Although to different degrees and in varying ways, all these countries have struggled with economic issues and have been subject to special attention by EU institutions, even when not obliged to be bailed-out and consequently to sign and implement a Memorandum of Understanding (MoU) with the so-called Troika (International Monetary Fund – IMF, European Central Bank – ECB, and European Commission). As we speculated in the first stage of the research, the latter situation has proven to be a relevant variable in the evolution of the national coordination management and regulation.

The research addressed the changes in the political and administrative system of each country that have occurred since the outbreak of the financial crisis in order to understand which of them are a result of the crisis and which are mostly linked to internal dynamics. Several factors may directly or indirectly affect the legal framework and concrete performance of each of the executives in the European realm, such as the size of the State and the corresponding administration and, more generally, the political ambition concerning EU policies. Recently, other elements have also had a strong impact on the organization of the executives, among them the willingness to play an active role in the management of the crisis, the need to increase the administrative capacity and the competence of national officials, as well as the kind of relations to be pursued with other Member States and the EU institutions.

The interdisciplinary perspective adopted combines the doctrinal reconstruction of the regulation concerning EU coordination with a practical analysis. The intention is to provide a constitutional and legal assessment of the issue, capable of integrating the political-science examinations present in the majority of former studies on coordination (particularly, Kassim, Peters, and Wright 2000) and to link this topic to the specific context of the financial crisis.

2 Traditional EU coordination between convergence and divergence until the crisis

Throughout the decades, the mechanisms and institutions created in each State to address the need for coordination have shown both patterns of convergence and divergence (Kassim, Peters and Wright 2000; Wessels and Mittag 2003; Goetz and Meyer-Sahling 2008). Although Europeanization of the administrations calls for more uniformity, national specificities and traditions still play a major role in the organization of domestic institutions.

The pressure for convergence stems from the fact that Member States act in an identical environment and have to face similar challenges when they prepare and then defend their position at the European level (Mény, Muller and Quermonne 1996). All governments have had to arrange their structures accordingly. Nevertheless, the need to adapt national structures to make them more responsive to the decision-making process in Brussels creates incentives towards similar coordination mechanisms, but, as the EU does not specify any such adaptations, the States are left with room to manoeuvre. The logic of optimization, which should have led to increasingly analogous processes and structures (Harmsen 1999, 84), has not become predominant.

At the national level, numerous characteristics of the domestic polity have been considered as influential, particularly the policy style, the conception of coordination, the nature of the political opportunity structure, and the administrative opportunity structure (Kassim 2000, 250 ff.). Additionally, the overall approach of the State towards the EU affects the focus of the coordination on implementing and/or influencing the decisions taken at the European level. Finally, the model of coordination adopted for internal affairs has an impact on the instruments used to achieve the same goal in EU-related issues.

The main similarities include: a) the establishment of new structures and/or adaptation of the pre-existing ones – a phenomenon that has occurred in both the long-term Member States and the most recent ones; b) the increasing role of the Prime Minister (PM); and c) the progressive erosion of the position of the Minister for Foreign Affairs (already highlighted by Kassim 2000, 239). On the one hand, technical issues require different skills from mainly diplomatic preparation; on the other hand, the expanding relevance of financial, monetary, and economic issues has pushed forward the role of the Ministries of Finance or Economy. This trend has been much stronger since the outbreak of the crisis.

Among the main differences are: a) the number of actors involved in the EU coordination (PM, ministers, Parliaments, Regions); b) the role that each of them plays in the process of coordination according to the domestic division of responsibilities; and c) the concrete mechanisms created and the way in which they function.

It is also possible to identify both commonalities and differences in the evolution of the EU coordination mechanisms in the years since the crisis. The following conclusions build on the findings of all the chapters included in this volume regarding the kind of adaptation that the crisis has brought about in terms of centralization/decentralization and long/short-lasting changes (see § 3). The role of the different actors involved, i.e. Prime Minister (PM), Ministry of Finance (MF), Ministry of Foreign Affairs (MFA) and Parliament, is explained from a comparative perspective (see § 4).

3 EU coordination in times of crisis: general characters of convergence

3.1 The adaptation of the domestic EU coordination has been mainly based on adjustments of the existing system

The process of EU coordination tended to accord a more relevant role to existing bodies, such as the Interministerial EU Committee (CIAE) in Italy and the General-Directorate for European Affairs (DGAE) in Portugal – where new legislation was passed to improve its participation in the policy-making process, with special attention to economic coordination in relation to the European Semester. In Ireland and Greece, the State responded to the crisis within the operating procedures of the political and administrative culture.

In Italy, the CIAE was reformed in 2012, but its structure and basic targets remained untouched. What changed was the frequency of its meetings. Although it had been statutorily regulated in 2005, for several years the coordination was performed through informal meetings of ministers. Only the appointment, in 2014, of Sandro Gozi (currently Secretary of State for European Affairs), who had been one of the promoters of the reform, determined the change. The first meetings of the Committee were held in June 2014 and they occur every three/four weeks.

In the Greek case, the system evolved according to the traditional state capacities and institutional organization: the changes were slow and initially based on merely *ad hoc* practices or even on personal informal arrangements. Only later were the structures around the Ministry of Finance (MF) amended slightly. Initially, the Secretary General of the MF held periodical information meetings and was in charge of the coordination of the affected ministries. When it had to monitor the implementation of the Memorandum of Understanding (MoU), the MF also made use of the Council of Economic Experts (the so-called SOE: see § 4.2) – whose role switched from think tank to actor of the management of EU issues, the General Secretariat of Economic Policy, and, more specifically, its EU Directorate. Only when the Troika explicitly requested a specialized structure with permanent technical personnel in 2011 did the legislature amend the coordination mechanism regulating a monitoring body for the structural adjustment programme: the Service for the Planning and Monitoring of the Implementation of Economic Adjustment Programmes, attached to the MF, was finally operative in 2013. The same year also saw the creation of a new mechanism of general coordination as a response to the requirements of a MoU: the General Secretariat for Coordination, attached to the PM and headed by a political appointee.

Portugal, where the emphasis was put on efficiency and the improvement of economic performance, faced a similar situation. Traditionally, the country has been portrayed as a Member State focused on downloading EU policies, which is surely true for the reform packages agreed upon with the Troika – a package that can be considered an example of 'coercive Europeanization' (Magone 2016). New legislation was passed to improve the participation of the DGAE – the main coordination body – in the policy-making process, with special attention to economic coordination for the European Semester. Within the DGAE, the Interministerial Commission of European Affairs (CIAE) was given a new statutory regulation in 2012; however, this regulation merely improved its efficiency and did not affect the structure. Nevertheless, a special taskforce was created to fulfil the tasks and the timing fixed by the MoU (the so-called ESAME, the Mission of Monitoring the Memoranda: see § 4.1).

The only exception to the pattern of adaptation of domestic mechanisms is inevitably Cyprus. When the country requested financial assistance in June 2012, it did not have in place any permanent structure capable of coordinating the negotiations with the Troika and monitoring the implementation of the MoU. There was just a European Affairs Deputy Minister appointed expressly for the Cypriot Presidency of the Council, whose mandate was supposed to end after the Presidency itself and did not include any participation in policy areas. In 2013, the coordination mechanism implemented in the MF reused the existing units and departments to create an efficient mechanism to communicate with the Troika.

3.2 Coercion from Europe has led to temporary changes at the domestic level

In the early 2000s, coercion was not considered a relevant factor for homogeneity among the States (Kassim 2000, 243). In the context of the financial crisis, however, the external push for coordination has played a bigger role due to the need to comply in a timely manner with the requirements of the MoU in the particularly weak economic situation of the affected countries. Loan conditionalities always implied the implementation of a specific set of policies, which changed the domestic priorities.

More specifically, the Economic Adjustment Programmes (EAP) that Greece agreed with the Troika in 2010 and 2012 and the one concerning the European Stability Mechanism (ESM) in 2015 prioritized some financial, fiscal, economic, and structural policies. Both the schedule and the deadline were extremely tight and complex to fulfil, requiring an expedited mechanism for the implementation of the reforms.

Nevertheless, the externally imposed changes seem to remain mainly temporary and, frequently, only partially effective. For instance, in Ireland, immediately after the elections in 2016, the PM decided to dissolve the Economic Management Council (EMC) that had been created to tackle the crisis (see §§ 4.1 and 4.2). In Portugal too, the aforementioned ESAME was established as a temporary taskforce in charge of coordinating the implementation of the programme. In Cyprus, the Government established at the end of 2013 that the EU Division within the MFA would be allotted the task of interministerial coordination of EU affairs; however, this new body rarely meets. In contrast, the internally driven changes that took place in Italy reflect the will to provide for long-lasting mechanisms of coordination. Chaired by a Secretary of State to the PM, ESAME remained small and flexible, ensured the flow of information with correspondents in the ministries as well as Parliament, and managed the channels of communications with the Troika. Since ESAME was of a temporary nature and dissolved once the programme had successfully been implemented, no major permanent institutional changes had been made to the basic structure of EU policy coordination, except for adding the task of economic coordination in relation to the European Semester to the DGAE in the policy-making process.

3.3 The reforms have contributed to the centralization of EU coordination

A shared pattern in the management of the crisis has been the centralization of EU policy coordination in the domestic arena.

In Ireland, the Government and the central administration became the 'domi-nant carrier of Europeanization', especially in the years when it was a programme country (2010–2013). In Portugal, the coordination of the Economic and Financial Adjustment Programme (EFAP) agreed upon with the Troika in 2011 was taken care of by the MF in cooperation with the Office of the PM.

In the Greek case, decentralization, fragmentation, and informality had been the longstanding features of EU coordination. Several ministries had traditionally been allotted a high degree of autonomy and the overall coordination had been conceived as a negative process based on a bottom-up mechanism. The need for positive coordination arose from the necessity to comply with the implementation of the reforms within the timetables and conditions set in the MoUs. As a result, there has been a (slow) phenomenon of centralization with different main actors: the agreements were usually arranged by the PM, the President of the SOE (Council of Economic Experts, attached to the MF), and the Minister of Finance, who then submitted the decisions for the approval of the Council of Ministers.

In Italy, the increasingly protagonist role of the PM in EU policy coordination was endorsed by the financial situation of the country, but this was not what triggered it. In fact, the importance of the PM in this field is the result of a process connected to the growing relevance of European affairs in internal politics and to the role of the PM as the representative of the State in the European Council.

Adopting the categories recently used by Kassim, i.e. a selective/compre-hensive and centralized/decentralized approach to EU policies, both Ireland and Portugal have a selective and centralized management of EU affairs (Kassim 2015). In Greece, the system moved from 'decentralized and selective' to 'centralized and selective' due to the tasks given to the MF. Lacking a per-manent body for coordination, Cyprus is still to be classified as a country with a decentralized system: even during the crisis, the executive mainly relied upon *ad hoc* arrangements. Italy kept its comprehensive approach in spite of the financial situation, yet also switched towards centralization having long been considered to have a decentralized model with different actors and veto players; but this change was mostly due to internal political dynamics.

4 The balance of power at the domestic level

4.1 Rising stars I: the Prime Ministers and their Offices

Overall, there have been several internal and external factors that have pushed towards an increasing importance of the PM, especially the growing importance of the European Council in EU policy-making. During the crisis, the co-ordination tasks of the PM and their Offices have been strengthened. Even in Portugal, where the MFA is still a very relevant actor, the temporary taskforce (ESAME) put in place to coordinate the implementation of the MoU was situated close to the Office of the PM.

In Greece, the PM had traditionally been strong politically but had exercised few coordination tasks, while the Deputy PM in charge of monitoring the coordination had also played a minor role. Nevertheless, between 2010 and 2012, the Office of the PM was transformed into a General Secretariat and was provided with a 'Strategic Planning Unit' (focused on the implementation of the reforms) and an 'EU and International Relations Office' (with broader tasks). Moreover, the General Secretariat of the Government (GSG) included an Office for International and Community Issues in 2010.

While only *ad hoc* committees have been arranged in Greece, the Irish Government has established some more stable bodies, among them an EU Committee composed of personnel from the ministries and a high-level Committee composed of ministers and senior civil servants, serviced by the Office of the PM. In any case, these two committees still depend on the political will of the PM to be convoked, since they have not completely been formalized. In general terms, the Irish Office of the PM is paramount in the management of EU-related issues and has established the strategic direction and focus for the European approach of the country. During the crisis, the PM and the Deputy PM were both members of the aforementioned Economic Management Council (EMC), which comprised the four most senior ministers of the core executive (see § 4.2), and the PM appointed another Secretary General to the Office of the PM in order to monitor the EMC. Progressively, the responsibility for core EU policy shifted from the MFA to the Office of the PM, which reduced the role of the MFA in the core executive. The MFA retained some responsibility but the Office of the PM became the nerve centre of the high politics of the Troika and the European Council.

In Italy as well, the Office of the PM has been transformed into the major coordination venue since the late 1980s, with the establishment of the Department for Coordination of Community Policies in 1987 (today Department for European Policies, DEP) and the corresponding Minister or Secretary of State for European Affairs. The DEP has always been attached to the Office of the PM and charged with coordinating EU policies in collaboration with other bodies also located there: the Interministerial EU Committee (CIAE) and the Technical Evaluation Committee (CTV) (Ragone 2014).

In the Italian case, the strengthening of the PM's role during the crisis was due to the new comprehensive approach to European affairs undertaken by the Italian Government and, in particular, by Matteo Renzi who became PM in

2014. This approach was accompanied by the target of improving the Italian performance in the ascending phase.

The attitude, personal skills, and political background of the PM in other cases also had an impact on the coordination mechanisms arranged within the executive. If it is partially true with respect to Portugal, it is clearly visible in the statements of the SYRIZA-led majority elected in Greece in 2015, which changed the existing system to purposefully create different levels of negotiations with the creditors.

4.2 Rising stars II: the Minister of Finance and/or the Minister of Economic Affairs

Alongside the PM, the second member of the core executive whose role has progressively been extended is the Minister of Finance and/or Economy; this has been increasingly the case since the start of the Single Market programme, the creation of EU structural and cohesion funds, and the Economic and Monetary Union (EMU) in the 1990s.

In Italy, there has been no recent formal change in the structure or tasks of the Ministry of Economy and Finance (MEF); however, its status has *de facto* was raised during the crisis due to the priority of economic and financial issues and the need to respond to European and international pressure with regard to austerity measures and spending cuts. In Portugal, the MF (in collaboration with the Office of the PM) also undertook the major part of the reforms and measures related to economic issues.

In Greece, the Council of Economic Experts (the SOE) had already been established in 1987 as a body with an advisory role in economic policy attached to the Ministry of Economic Affairs (MEA). During the crisis, the MEA was reorganized, but the reforms depended on domestic factors: in particular, it was separated from the MF in 2009 (with which it had been merged seven years earlier), and the realm of economic and development policies is now divided between the two ministries. Despite this shared competence, only the MF has overseen the implementation of the MoU, as it is also in contact with the Troika and the other Eurozone Member States. The MF inaugurated a new model of coordination that was more concentrated and effective than the one led by the MFA.

In Ireland, the MF has gone through a structural change as well: in 2011, it was split into the Ministry of Public Expenditure and Reform and the MF, respectively in charge of the reforms to be implemented and the traditional financial issues. These two ministers were also members of the new Economic Management Council (EMC), which was set up (temporarily) by the Government and became the main strategic centre of coordination in the management of the crisis. The PM and the Deputy PM were the other two members of the ECM.

In Cyprus too, the MF was designated as the leading actor of the coordination when, in 2013, the executive established an interministerial Committee in charge of implementing the reforms. Furthermore, a few months later the bureaucratic management was transferred from the Planning Bureau of the MFA to the Unit of Strategic Coordination and Cooperation, both units falling under the MF.

4.3 Falling stars: the Ministries of Foreign Affairs (with a stable role of the Permanent Representations)

The MFA has been a very relevant ministry since the beginning of European integration, especially during the early years after the accession of Member States, but it has generally entered a period of decline for several reasons. In Portugal, it is still very relevant, since it is the core seat for EU coordination – i.e. the DGAE and the Secretary of State of European Affairs are attached to the MFA. In Greece, the MFA had been in charge of the general coordination in a decentralized and negative manner for decades, but the MF, focusing on the implementation of MoU-obligations, inverted the model during the crisis. In Cyprus, by contrast, the Government decided in 2013 to charge the EU Division within the MFA with the responsibility for domestic coordination of EU policies. Under this arrangement, the politically highest level of coordination would supposedly take place in the Interministerial Committee for EU Affairs, which is chaired by the Minister of Foreign Affairs; moreover, the coordination between the officials of the different EU units of the ministries is also characterized by the leading role of the corresponding unit of the MFA.

In Ireland and Italy, the MFA was the lead ministry until the late 1980s and used to take care of the daily management of EU coordination; then, however, it had to share the task with the Office of the PM. More specifically, the Irish MFA monitors the developments at the EU level, aided by its privileged institutional and political position. It has a Europe Division, which determines the national position in collaboration with the EU Division of the Office of the PM, and a Political Division, which is responsible for the decisions related to the Common Foreign Security Policy and defence issues. The same can be said about the MFA of the other countries, which are still the most important players in that field.

In addition to being the main actor in this non-Europeanized policy, the MFA represents the institutional linkage with the Permanent Representation in Brussels, which has been described in all cases as an essential player for coordination and as a highly qualified body that comprises skilled and experienced personnel.

The Permanent Representation of most countries is a sort of miniature of the core executive. In the Irish case, the number of ministries has grown since the 1970s to the point that all of them (except for the Office of the PM) are now represented in Brussels. The Greek, the Portuguese, and the Italian Representations also include, in addition to the MFA diplomats and experts, representatives of all other ministries, who keep in contact, more or less informally, with their corresponding ministries at home. They also interact on a daily basis with the national coordination body, even in cases in which that body does not belong to the MFA. In the case of Cyprus, the Permanent Representation acts essentially as a mediator and is led by a career diplomat who receives instructions and indications from the MFA.

4.4 Fallen stars: Parliaments

European integration has determined the transfer of legislative matters from the domestic level to the supranational level, thereby also fostering an internal shift of power towards the executives, which represent the State within the EU institutions. Moreover, during the crisis the need to take decisions quickly has favoured the Governments involved in the summits and the meetings of the European Council and the Eurozone, as well as the frequent use of the intergovernmental method (Kjaer, Teubner and Febbrajo 2011; Tuori and Tuori 2013).

The executives have not only driven and coordinated anti-crisis policies outside national borders, but they have often manipulated the discourse internally, submitting to their corresponding Parliaments the measures agreed upon at the European level or with the Troika as a *fait accompli.* Parliaments tend to sanction such decisions, either because they are caught up in the 'saving the EU rhetoric' or because they are keen on being involved in budgetary and economic issues, even only *a posteriori* (Puntscher Riekmann and Wydra 2013, 565 ff.). In Cyprus, for instance, various opposition parties voted in favour of passing the crisis-related legislation out of responsibility, even though the Government had lost the parliamentary majority support at the beginning of 2014. In Greece, basically the only thing Parliament could do was ratify several decisions concerning anti-crisis measures that had been decided by the executive.

In Ireland, there has also been a progressive limitation of parliamentary involvement in EU matters during the crisis, although its scrutiny functions were improved in 2002 through the EU Scrutiny Subcommittee of the Joint Parliament Committee for European Affairs. A few years later (in 2006),

Portugal also granted the parliamentary Committee of European Affairs *ex ante* powers of scrutiny. In spite of its marginal role, the Italian Parliament, in comparison with the legislatures of the other countries most affected by the financial crisis, was considered to have been the most active in recent years (Auel and Höing 2014).

Bibliography

Auel K. and Höing O. (2014) 'Scrutiny in Challenging Times – National Parliaments in the Eurozone Crisis', *SIEPS European Policy Analysis* 1 (1–16).

Goetz K.H. and Meyer-Sahling J.-H. (2008) 'The Europeanisation of National Political Systems: Parliaments and Executives', *Living Reviews in European Governance* 3 (2) (4–30).

Harmsen, R. (1999), 'The Europeanization of National Administrations: A Comparative Study of France and the Netherlands', *Governance* 12 (1) (81–113).

Kassim H. (2000), 'Conclusion', in Kassim H., Peters B.G. and Wright V. (eds.), *The National Co-ordination of EU Policy. The Domestic Level*, Oxford, Oxford University Press (236–264).

Kassim H. (2015) 'The National Coordination of EU Policy', in Magone J. (ed.), *Routledge Handbook of European Politics*, London, Routledge (686–707).

Kassim H., Peters B.G. and Wright V. (eds.) (2000) *The National Co-ordination of EU Policy. The Domestic Level*, Oxford, Oxford University Press.

Kjaer P.K., Teubner G. and Febbrajo A. (eds.) (2011), *The Financial Crisis in Constitutional Perspective. The Dark Side of Functional Differentiation*, Oxford, Hart Publishing.

Magone J. (2016) 'Portugal as the "Good Pupil of the European Union". Living under the Regime of the Troika', in Magone J., Laffan B. and Schweiger C. (eds.), *Core-Periphery Relations in the European Union. Power and Conflict in a Dualist Political Economy*, London, Routledge (179–189).

Mény Y., Muller P. and Quermonne J.-L. (eds.) (1996) *Adjusting to Europe. The Impact of the European Union on National Institution and Policies*, London, Routledge.

Puntscher Riekmann S. and Wydra D. (2013) 'Representation in the European State of Emergency: Parliaments against Governments?', *Journal of European Integration* 35 (5) (565–582).

Ragone S. (2014) 'La coordinación gubernamental de las políticas europeas. Un análisis de derecho comparado sobre los miembros fundadores', *Estudios de Deusto* 61 (2) (213–234).

Tuori K. and Tuori K. (2013), *The Eurozone Crisis. A Constitutional Analysis*, Cambridge, Cambridge University Press.

Wessels W. and Mittag J. (2003) 'The "One" and the "Fifteen"? The Member States between Procedural Adaptation and Structural Revolution', in Wessels W., Mauer A. and Mittag J. (eds.), *Fifteen into One? The European Union and Its Member States*, Manchester, Manchester University Press.

Index

For Product Safety Concerns and Information please contact our EU representative GPSR@taylorandfrancis.com
Taylor & Francis Verlag GmbH, Kaufingerstraße 24, 80331 München, Germany

www.ingramcontent.com/pod-product-compliance
Ingram Content Group UK Ltd.
Pitfield, Milton Keynes, MK11 3LW, UK
UKHW011019180926
475701UK00004B/820
9780367875541